Help me, I'm Hurt

THE CHILD-ABUSE HANDBOOK

James R. Davis

**KENDALL/HUNT
PUBLISHING COMPANY**
Dubuque, Iowa

11/10/08

Copyright © 1982 by Kendall/Hunt Publishing Company

Library of Congress Catalog Card Number: 82–82375

ISBN 0–8403–2747–1

Printed in the United States of America

B   402747   01

"To you the children, may your weeping cease."

Contents

Foreword

"Times have changed, but abuse has not!" The willful and deliberate beating and whipping of children has remained with society for centuries. It has nearly become institutionalized within our familial framework, our educational system, and our religious heritage. Discipline has never been a bad thing; but abuse has never served any worthwhile purpose. The convergence of the two is not only disheartening but socially unacceptable.

The reform of our juvenile justice process the latter part of the nineteenth century, was not enough. The Society for the Prevention of Cruelty to Children was not enough in the early twentieth century. By the end of the first quarter of the 1900's, nothing substantive had really been done. Today the family court system is seriously overcrowded and overworked. In the decade of the 1960's, all fifty states codified laws relative to abuse. Many even required mandatory reporting of abuse by professionals entrusted with the care, recreation, and education of children. The outcome of all this statistically is staggering, we are faced with a contagion out of control.

The social ethic of our times hasn't failed, but has come close to it. There has never really been a bonafide effort to protect children from parents, guardians, live-in surrogate parents, and the elite.

Rather, we have seen the domination of a theme called "protection of society." Are children constantly beaten, burned, boiled, cut, raped, sexually exploited, and sold, not part of our society? These past few years have been exciting. We have seen the emergence of an interest never equaled at anytime before in our history to respond to the problems of abuse, incest, and molestation. The proactive movement has arrived. We are all entrusted with a responsibility. Let us affirm to continue to strive to eradicate the insidious social problem of abuse to children.

L. O. Giuffrida
F. J. Villella

Crimes against children include the following:

1. Physical Assault (non-accidental injury)

2. Sexual Assault

3. Emotional/Mental Deprivation

4. Physical Neglect (unfit home)

Introduction

During the last ten years there has not only been an alarming increase in the incidence of child abuse and neglect cases; but a growing interest in examination, reformation, and education related to the child as victim.

While a significant number of nations in the world have thought of themselves as child-loving and child-caring, there is an increasing indication based on scientific study, that this is not the case.

For example, quoting from an article which appeared in one of the more reputable journals on the subject, we can clearly identify a universal phenomenon in the United States.[1]

- While the child population in America is decreasing, a larger percentage of children live in poverty today than in 1970. One out every four American children under age 18 lives in poverty—a total of 17 million children.
- Three-fourths of the 1,700 mentally retarded children in America live in slums. Less than 10 percent of the children affected with mental health problems receive help.
- The United States ranks after 16 other nations in infant mortality rates.
- Addiction and alcoholism among children is nearing epidemic proportions with fewer services being offered to combat the problem.
- Teenage pregnancies are on a dramatic increase. Some estimate that in the United States one million women under 18 would conceive during 1977 and that 60 percent of them would give birth. At the same time, venereal diseases—gonorrhea in particular—have reached epidemic proportions among the young as well. The amount of funds allocated to effectively tackle these problems is minimal.
- As many as one million children under age six suffer from malnutrition or outright starvation which affect not only the children's physical growth but the brain growth as well. The fact

1. Victimology-An International Journal—see footnote #3.

that malnutrition is linked with low school achievement and therefore with low learning potential has serious implications for any society.

- Every year there are over 60,000 reported cases of child abuse and neglect. Over 16,000 children die each year from neglect and abuse, the second most common cause of death for small children.
- More than half the crime in America is committed by minors, with few treatment and rehabilitation services available as an alternative to jail-like detention. Some people feel that the juvenile justice system has virtually broken down. At the same time, violence is portrayed and glorified in countless television programs watched by millions of children every day.[2]
- Over 2 million children are arrested each year, many for status offenses. Young offenders are often detained under vague statutes in adult jails, sometimes alongside hard-core criminals. Maltreatment, assault, sexual abuse often victimize both male and female detainees.
- Thousands of children are needlessly deprived of a good home because adoption procedures are so complicated that would-be adoptive parents can't cope with the red tape. Youngsters in foster care suffer because they are often bounced from home to home, with little regard for their spiritual and emotional well-being.
- Many children are sexually assaulted by adults in positions of authority, trust and care, even by their own parents or guardians. The incidence of juvenile sexual victimization is unknown. "Best guess" estimates have been made—among others—by the American Humane Association (AHA): 3,000 cases of child sexual victimization in large urban areas annually (AHA, 1976); a national average of 5,000 cases of father-daughter incest (AHA, 1968); and 200,000 cases of sexual offenses on female children age 4 to 14 years (AHA, 1968). Studies indicate that in an overwhelming majority of cases, the offender is not a stranger, but someone familiar to the child or his/her family. Although still surrounded by strong societal taboos, incest cases are increasingly being brought to light.

2. In June 1977, Rep. G. Vander Jagt introduced legislation in the Congress of the United States—House Resolution 604—calling for the investigation of the relationship between TV violence and violent behavior of children and adults.

- Exploitation of children is practiced worldwide, notwithstanding the laws to the contrary. Children of migrant workers join their parents or caretakers for long, exhausting hours in the field to pick fruits and vegetables for meager wages. Around the world, children are still being sold into slavery or servitude.[3]

There are of course, many many areas of victimization of children that could have been and maybe should have been included in the writing. It is however, quite possible that we would have ended up with such a voluminous work; that it simply would not have been as useful.

As Dr. Ray Helfer and Dr. C. Henry Kempe have so aptly put it, "Children are indeed brought up in a world of abnormal rearing."[4] Evidence confirms this, and in anticipation, rather than attempting to improve parenting, we have suggested a "Recognition, Reporting, and Response Model," which should prove helpful in stemming the tide of cases in this area confronting law enforcement, public education, and public health agencies across the country.

Most characterizations and aspects of child abuse response in our society are based on unfounded data and little comprehension of the magnitude of the problem. In 1974, the Child Abuse Prevention and Treatment Act became law and established the National Center on Child Abuse and Neglect. In California, in 1977, quoting the Child Abuse Information Pamphlet No. 8, California Department of Justice, 72,000 cases of child maltreatment were reported. This is only one state's statistics; imagine the magnitude when multiplied by fifty, not to mention the cases which are not reported.

Today, that figure in California has doubled, and nationally, there are in excess of one million cases of abuse, which although an estimation, probably quite low, if reporting criterion is the indicator. Some agencies have noted that a ratio of three or four cases to one, go unreported. If this is the case, we are amidst an epidemic that is so insidious as to render the public's attitude "speechless." We may have millions of cases, not simply a single million cases!

What are we talking about? What are the warning signs? Who can help? Can we assist battering individuals and their victims? In reality, we have the ability if collective social action intervention is implemented uniformly, to eradicate a goodly portion of the problem.

3. VICTIMOLOGY: An International Journal—Volume 2, Number 2, Summer 1977, pp. 175–180—Copyright 1977 Visage Press, Inc. Printed in U.S.A.
4. Ibid.

Effective multi-disciplinary action can only result if there is basic agreement on a conceptual teamwork approach. Child protection workers, police and probation officers, dentists and members of the medical profession (medical social workers, nurses, examining physicians, pediatricians, and pediatric radiologists) can be trained to identify the problem, verify the case, proceed with treatment, as well as, prosecution if need be, and eventually respond therapeutically to the entire family. Elementary and secondary teachers are an excellent source of detection, response, and assistance.

Lack of knowledge still remains the major problem in effecting a long range strategy. There can be no professional jealousy, no petty "specialist chauvinism," and no limiting of interprofessional and paraprofessional contact among those entrusted with response and resolution.

Before we can fully understand our responsibility and opportunity, we need to be familiar with our possible involvement. The California legislature by one of their most recent amendments to law, has made it clear in the California Penal Code, that all persons working with children have a responsibility to care for their welfare. Ideally, this type of "Reporting Statute" could be implemented in every state in the United States. This is a first step in the right direction. It is important to remember though, that reporting should be considered proactive and within the context of a "helping response," not a punitive lever.

Chapter 1

Child Abuse Is . . .

Child abuse is any act of omission or commission that endangers or impairs a child's physical or emotional health and development. This includes: physical assault, corporal punishment, emotional assault, emotional deprivation, physical neglect or inadequate supervision and sexual exploitation. Simply put, *non-accidental injury.*

The infliction of injury, *rather than the degree,* is the determinant for intervention. Detecting initially inflicted small injuries and intervening with preventative action may save a child from further permanent injury or death.

Children are frequently subject to deplorable home conditions wherein their physical and psychological needs are not met. As police officers, we are responsible for the safety and welfare of the minor. The need for protecting children is magnified because of their inability to control or sometimes even to recognize their situation.

Child abuse is a leading cause of infant mortality in the United States. It is estimated that nearly one million American children are suffering from abuse and/or neglect at any given time. Approximately one quarter of those million children will be permanently injured for life as a result of being maltreated. Medical experts in the field of child abuse pretty much agree that the size of intensity of the injury is not representative of the danger that the child is in. As in many cases of child beating, the next beating may be the last for the child.

In California, more than 72,000 cases of suspected child maltreatment were reported to child protective services agencies in 1977. It is estimated, however, that only about one-fifth of the actual cases are reported.

Assessing family emotional relationships is a critical aspect of child abuse procedures. When observing a family, it is important to be fully aware of personal biases and preconceptions and to be able to differentiate between practices of childrearing which are truly harmful to children and those practices which merely reflect different lifestyles.

A parent/caretaker may not be aware that what they did is against the law. Sometimes the cultural background or religious belief cause him/her to treat the minor(s) in a manner that, although causing injury (mental and/or physical), was not committed in a "tortuous manner" or with malice.

While there appears to be serious under-reporting to the Department of Justice's statewide child abuse index as required by law, the following percentages of those cases that have been reported are revealing. Of the cases reported in calendar year 1977:

44.2% were physical abuse
21.3% were in the "general neglect" category
34.5% were sexual abuse

The age distribution factors from 1977 reveal:

Physical Abuse and General Neglect

0– 4 years—*heaviest incidence*
5– 8 years—less, but still heavy
9–16 years—begins to diminish
16–up   —diminishes sharply

Sexual Abuse

0– 4 years—less than 5–8 and 13–16
5– 8 years—slightly less than 9–12
9–12 years—*heaviest incidence*
13–16 years—slightly less than 9–12
16–up   —diminished sharply

The serious and pervasive problem of child abuse and neglect is recognized and dealt with by a variety of disciplines. Laws have been passed and are enforced, medical diagnostic techniques discovered, counseling offered and direct services provided to families in difficulty. However, none of the strategies alone can effectively combat child maltreatment. We must all be concerned with the detection, treatment and, above all, the effective prevention of child abuse and neglect.

In the end, there are really three victims of child abuse—the child, the perpetrator(s) and the community. We, as observers, are the invaluable "third party" so necessary for the protection of children of any age—and specifically for the protection of those human beings too young to protect themselves.

The problem of child abuse in our society, if ignored, assures a continuing pattern of violence and crime. It is a documented fact that those who are violent towards others were themselves, almost invariably, victims of abuse. Abused children grow up to abuse. Contrary to popular belief, child abuse occurs in all cultural, ethnic, occupational and socio-economic groups. There is a proportionately higher incidence of abuse *reported* in minority and low-income families, but it is also true that these families have more contact with agencies who have legal reporting responsibilities established by Section 11161.5 of the California Penal Code.

Statistics show that many of the battering parents were battered children themselves. Consequently, these parents use the same destructive techniques on their children as their parents practiced on them. Without intervention, these negative patterns are transmitted for generations. They have learned early in life that having had harm inflicted on them by supposedly those that love them most, that is, their parents, violence must be equatable with love. As a result, the battered child often becomes a battering "Mommy" or "Daddy."

The Battering Parent Syndrome

A battering parent is one who fits into one or more of the following categories:
1. An individual simply repeating the type of discipline or child management to which he was subjected as a child.
2. An individual who, as a child, has been shunted from foster home to foster home and feels rejected.
3. An individual who exhibits significant lack of identity and poor self-concept or self-image.
4. Parents who are hostile, abusive, impetuous and who lash out at insignificant things frequently and react in a hairtriggered manner.

The battering parents' *behavior* often demonstrates in their feeling an overwhelming:
1. Disorganization, disorder, worthlessness and lack of self-esteem.
2. Apathy, lethargy, depression and neglect of their own physical health.
3. Need for quick, impulsive gratifications without concern for consequences or others in general.
4. Competitiveness with their children in which they play to win, not for fun or instruction.
5. A tendency to blame others.

3

6. A conviction that their needs are being disregarded and attacked by society which is always commanding them to do better.
7. Sense of abandonment and punishment by their own parents, and a longing for a parent.
8. Self-centeredness.

Some attitudes of battering parents when confronted with suspicions of battery are:

1. Little concern, guilt or remorse regarding the child's battered condition.
2. A show of fear or anger at being asked for an explanation of the injuries.
3. Evasive or contradictory statements about the circumstances of the mistreatment whether it be emotional or physical.
4. Placing blame on the child for any injuries.
5. Continual criticism of the child and little to say in a positive way about the child.
6. Viewing the child's injuries or problems as an assault on themselves and their abilities.
7. Lack of touching or looking at the child and their failures to respond or inappropriate response to the child.
8. Disregard for and minimization of the child's needs and behavior, and no perception of how a child can feel.
9. A guilt over and/or an expectation of another failure.
10. Cooperation based on fear for themselves rather than concern for the child while they try to conceal as much as possible.

The battering parents' behavior often demonstrates their actions:

1. An overly suspicious, defensive, evasive, negative, underdog attitude toward authority.
2. A lonely, seclusive, curtain-drawn type of life. They have no real friends although they may have a number of acquaintances.
3. The use of infants and children to satisfy their love needs.
4. A search for social satisfaction from their child which the child cannot fulfill.
5. The punishment of the child when he cannot satisfy the parents' impossible demands.
6. The tendency to move frequently whenever the neighborhood suspects them of abuse.

4

7. The need for frequent changes of doctors or hospitals to protect themselves from suspicion.
8. A flight from life by drinking or drugs.

Interest has recently been focused on the degree of stress placed upon families and the lack of security created by the difficulties in obtaining the basic necessities of life including food, shelter, clothing, medical care and education. It is believed that parents under such stress may be less capable of providing adequately for the emotional needs of their children. In struggling for survival, such a parent may be incapable of resolving stressful situations rationally. In such situations, clashes with children would be likely.

Child abuse is seldom the result of any single factor. Rather it is a combination of circumstances as well as personality types which precipitates acts of child abuse.

The child abuser is typically a recidivist; that is, the abuser tends to repeat the abuse. The abuser is also typically an escalator in that the amount of and severity of the abuse tends to increase. Because of these typical characteristics, early identification, reporting and intervention are essential and vital. There is help for the battered child and the battering parent; but it is a community problem.

Chapter 2

Types of Child Abuse

The most common cause of inflicted injury is overpunishment which occurs when corporal punishment is unreasonably severe. This usually happens when the parent is extremely agitated or angry, and either throws, or strikes the child too hard or continues to beat him.

"Discipline and punishment are not the same thing! Discipline seeks to guide; which is not the case with punishment. Parents and child need to establish mutual respect and rules of behavior."*

Reportable suspected child abuse would generally fall into the following categories:

1. Any injury unusual for a specific age group, i.e., any fracture in an infant.
2. History of previous recurrent injury.
3. Unexplained injury—unable to explain; discrepancies in given explanation, blame placed on third party, explanation inconsistent with medical diagnosis, etc.
4. Excessive bruising in an area other than unusual traumatic contact (described in detail later).
5. Evidence of no or poor supervision.
6. Evidence of neglect (described later).
7. Any indication of sexual abuse (described later).
8. Verbal threats against the life of a child made by parent(s) or guardian.

Physical Assault and Corporal Punishment

While there are many who feel that all corporal punishment is abusive, there are many others who feel it useful under *restrained* conditions as a method of discipline.

---

*During the proof-reading my wife offered this statement, which bears repeating. My thanks and love to you Cecelia.

7

Basically, the clinical signs of physical abuse are as follows: Evidence of bodily injury, bruises, abrasions, cuts, lacerations, burns, soft tissue swelling, hematoma, dislocation, fracture, etc. Intentional, deliberate assault or otherwise torturing a child is included in this category of child abuse.

Detecting physical assault: Physical abuse is "suspected" when any of the following occurs:

Bruises—The most common injuries are bruises. Bruises may be accidentally inflicted during normal play or activity. *Nonaccidental* bruises generally:

- are on multiple planes of the body at the same time—indicating that the child has been hit from different directions;
- posterior planes of the body: buttocks, backs of thighs, legs, arms, head, etc.;
- have a pattern, i.e., palm or finger prints, buckle prints, parallel linear marks caused by belts, cords, etc.;
- repetitive bruises of varying ages (color indicates age of bruise);
- odd shapes and sizes of injuries;
- injuries under clothing—school-age children especially.

The timing or age dating (ecchymoses) of bruises can be an important factor. The following are approximations, but can be used as a rough guide:

Time Inflicted	Color of Bruise
Immediate—few hours	Red
Soon—6 to 12 hours	Blue
Later—12 to 24 hours	Black-purple
4 to 6 days	Green tint, dark
5 to 10 days	Pale green to yellow

Burns—Burns are often very difficult to evaluate. Many burns, however, are characteristic of abuse in that they appear to have the shape of a recognizable object evenly burned into the skin, indicating prolonged contact.

Burns which have been inflicted *nonaccidentally* generally:

- glove or sock-like appearance on hands and feet from immersion in hot liquid;
- donut shape on buttocks—held down in hot liquid;
- pointed or deeper in middle—hot liquid poured on;

8

- shape of object—poker, heater grille, utensil, etc.
- searing effect with charring around the wound—usually multiple from cigarette.

Bones/Fractures—"No explanation" of why the child has the fracture is a cause for suspicion that it is a *nonaccidental* injury.
- any fracture in an infant under 12 months is suspect;
- spiral fractures—long bones (arms and legs) fractures that are the result of twisting are almost always due to inflicted trauma.

Other—Other indications that physical abuse may be "suspected" is when:
- child generally fearful of adults, non-spontaneous, refuses to speak in front of parents;
- or conversely, child *overly eager* to please adults when asked to perform menial tasks;
- parents over-react and are extremely nervous;
- parents bring child to medical facility for unneeded treatment;
- very young children with injuries on the back surfaces of the body from the neck to the knees. This is a primary target zone and the largest percentage of injuries are directed to this area.
- bruises, scars and wounds on the back of arms and hands which are characterized as "defense" wounds;
- excessive layers of clothing, especially in hot weather, should arouse curiosity since clothing may be hiding wounds.

Emotional Assault

Just as physical injuries can scar and incapacitate a child, emotional cruelty can similarly cripple and handicap a child. Excessive verbal assaults, i.e., belittling, blaming, sarcasm, unpredictable responses, continual negative moods, constant family discord, and double message communication are examples of ways parents may inflict emotional abuse upon the child.

Emotional assault is "suspected" if:

- child is very withdrawn, depressed and apathetic;
- child "acts out," is considered a "behavior problem";
- child displays other signs of emotional turmoil such as repetitive, rhythmic movements; inordinate attention to details; no verbal or physical communication with others, etc.

9

Emotional Deprivation

Emotional deprivation has been defined as ". . . the deprivation suffered by children when their parents/caretakers do not provide the normal experiences producing feelings of being loved, wanted, secure and worthy."[5]

For normal development, children need emotional involvement from their parents/caretakers as much as they need proper nutrition. Infants who do not experience any affection are subject to mortality in spite of the physical needs being met. Emotional starvation is one of the most difficult types of abuse to detect and is perhaps the most tragic.

Emotional deprivation is "suspected" if the following are observed:

- child refuses to eat or eats little, and is very frail;
- child not thriving in general;
- "anti-social" behavior, i.e., aggression disruption, etc.;
- "delinquent" behavior, i.e., drug abuse, vandalism, etc.;
- excessively seeks-out and "pesters" other adults for attention and affection.

Physical Neglect

Physical neglect is the failure of a parent/caretaker to provide a child with adequate food, shelter, clothing, protection, supervisions and medical and dental care.

Physical neglect is "suspected" if the following conditions exist:

- unsanitary conditions in home, i.e., garbage, animal or human excretion, etc.
- lack of heating in home;
- fire hazards in home;
- sleeping arrangements cold or dirty or otherwise inadequate;
- infestation of insects or rodents in home;
- nutritional quality of food in home poor;
- meals not prepared;
- spoiled food in refrigerator or cupboards;
- child lacking in medical or dental care;
- child always sleepy or hungry;

---

5. Defined by: Robert M. Mulford, a member of the National Advisory Committee of the Children's Division, American Humane Association.

- clothing always dirty or inadequate for weather;
- child under 14 years left alone in home or unsupervised for long periods of time.

Sexual Exploitation/Molestation/Incest

Sexual molestation of children within the family is the least talked about type of child abuse. Because of its taboo nature and the difficulty of observation, it is largely unreported and some researchers feel it may be even more common than physical abuse.

Sexual abuse occurs to infants and children of all ages, but more frequently to girls. In many instances, the mother is aware that sexual activity is taking place. The sexual activity is usually repeated until the child is old enough and determined enough to gain attention outside the family. The act could be transferred to child number two and number three.[6]

The assault is typically non-violent. The offender doesn't see himself as doing harm to the child. However gentle or forceful the approach may be, it happens only when the child is alone and defenseless, and it is followed by guilt-provoking demands for secrecy and threats of terrible harm if the secret is broken.

It should be obvious that incestuous (or intrafamilial) assault is an exploitation of the availability and trusting obedience of a child who looks to a parent or guardian for love, security and guidance. While it is often deceptively non-violent, it is more powerfully compelling and more totally disabling than any strongarm attack from a stranger.

Sexual exploitation is "suspected" if one or more of the following is present:

- the child reports sexual activities with parents;
- the child shows an early and exaggerated awareness of sex, with either seductive interest or fearful avoidance in close contact with others;
- there is tearing, bruising or specific inflammation of the mouth, anus, or genitals, or evidence of semen (oral, vaginal, rectal).
- the child "sexually" squirms.
- venereal disease of the eyes, mouth, anus, or genitals of a child under fifteen;

6. Commonly referred to as "transference" factor.

- a girl is pregnant and very evasive in naming her partner;
- a child is known to be the victim of other forms of abuse by parent(s).

Exploitation/Child Pornography

Child pornography is a form of child abuse for profit which appears to be a growing industry. Although it is impossible to make an exact assessment of the number of California children who have been the victims of this kind of sexual exploitation, it is clear that by even the most conservative estimate, the number is alarmingly high, approaching the tens of thousands.

The difficulty in fixing an exact estimate of the number of children involved is compounded by a number of factors. First, the evidence indicates that in the vast majority of cases, this kind of sexual exploitation goes unreported, even to the parents of the children. Additionally, the ever-increasing number of juvenile runaways who have migrated to California in recent years, together with the associated and growing problem of juvenile prostitution, contribute to the difficulty in making this assessment. Finally, there is evidence that some parents have used their own children to produce this material. Therefore, the only reasonable conclusion which can be drawn is that the number of children involved is substantial, and that the number appears to be growing.

Child Molesters and Chickenhawks

Contrary to what is perceived as forced sexual abuse or exploitation, as previously discussed, this section deals with child victims of sexual abuse who are usually consenting partners or noncomplaining victims.

The Los Angeles Police Department's Sexually Exploited Child Unit, which has been in operation for three years defines a "child molester" as male or female (but primarily an older adult male heterosexual) who receives gratification from young girls. A "Chickenhawk" is defined as a male (adult homosexual) or female who receives such gratification from young boys. The child molesters and chickenhawks usually have a specific age preference.

12

Chickenhawks and child molesters are "benevolent keepers" of their child victims. For the majority of their time together, the child's wants and needs are catered to by the suspect in an exaggerated caring relationship, in return for which the child willingly submits to sexual activity. While this perverse form of attention and affection may be especially appealing to an isolated runaway child, the danger is certainly not limited to runaways. It can and does represent a danger to a parent/child relationship where there is a failure by the parent(s) to provide necessary attention and affection.

Chapter 3

Can Abuse Be Alleviated?

After community members become aware of the broad scope of child abuse and child neglect, they will naturally wonder, and maybe even worry, about what to do next. A role model designed to answer their questions was developed and tested during the year of the children's rights project. Interdisciplinary vocabulary words were used so that persons of all vocations, professions, ages, or management levels could seek their role. Pertinent words and definitions are:

Observer: Anyone who sees conditions among individuals, groups, institutions, or society which may indicate abuse and/or neglect.

Perpetrator: Any one person, group, institution, or community that performs acts of commission or fails by acts of omission, thus blocking potential development of children.

Caretaker: Any parent, relative, friend, teacher, institutional personnel, or anyone else reponsible for a child.

Mediator: Any person, group, system, or change which can intervene to prevent, treat, or rehabilitate children, families, institutions, and/or communities. Some mediators are professionally trained to do this, but all persons may be involved.

Community: All persons within a geographical area—town, district, county, or state. Areas may overlap.

Now refer to the mode and begin with the observer. ANYONE who sees the situation or conditions of an abused or neglected child should TELL a mediator. Anyone, anywhere, anytime, may be an observer. The only way the child will be helped is to have the observer tell someone (mediator) about his or her observation. If the observer chooses a competent mediator who will follow through, the observer's role is over. For example, physicians, nurses, schoolteachers, day care workers, etc., may be observers. By telling the protective service worker (example of a professional mediator), the observer's role is completed.

Some mediators acquire their label informally—grandparents, motherly or fatherly neighbors, concerned citizens. Hopefully, they can define their own role and decide when another level of expertise is needed. The numbers of available professionally trained mediators will vary by geographical area. Each county should have a protective service worker, public health nurse, and mental health professional (or more than one). Voluntary agencies vary with population size. Each community is responsible for locating professionally trained mediators.

Whoever the mediator, he/she must immediately focus attention on the child and determine if the child is safe, potentially unsafe or unsafe. Once this major decision is made, the actions to be taken appear in the mode. At no time does the mediator drop the case after a cursory review. Several visits must be made to the family or situation site, and evaluations should be made over a period of time. All actions should be based on the child's safety, and the least detrimental alternative should be chosen.

If the child is unsafe, immediate investigation and removal of either the child or the perpetrator must occur. The child's condition may indicate hospitalization, or perhaps temporary foster care will be initiated. Several disciplines should be involved to deal with the child, the family, and the situation. After all facts are weighed and the least detrimental (to the child) alternative is chosen, permanent removal from the home may be proposed to the circuit court. This is rarely needed; alternatives would depend heavily on community services and long-term follow-up.

The child in a safe situation is by no means forgotten or left to his own or family's fate. The community is called upon to provide for the basic needs of the child and/or caretaker, to reverse indicators through information, education, and behavior change, and to promote child-adult interrelationships. The process occurs over many months or years.

The potentially unsafe child is in a precarious situation in that at any time, he/she may become unsafe. Frequent evaluations and close contact must be made by the mediator or a designee. At any time of unsafety, the removal route must be taken if the child remains within the situation, supportive services from the community must be used to strengthen the child-caretaker interrelationships.

So far the action model has been picturing a one-to-one situation where observer sees child and causes intervention by team planning and services individualized for that child. The damaging conditions or crisis have occurred, however, and the child will probably be at least emotionally scarred for life. The action is after the fact. How much better all children would develop if abuse and neglect were prevented.

The children's rights project as well as all other projects comes to the conclusion that prevention is the preferred route. Prevention is a total community commitment. The left side of the role model relates to the entire community for this reason. Four major areas of activity are mentioned, but the most basic is the first: define and promote children's rights.

Only when a community is willing to develop a consensus toward recognition of children as valuable human citizens rather than chattels of parents will true prevention of abuse and neglect be feasible. Hopefully this self-help manual will serve to initiate discussion and understanding of the vital premise.[7]

Children's Rights: Theory and Practice

The remediation and prevention of child abuse and neglect is not truly possible until children are guaranteed special and fundamental rights by the constitution and other legislation. Citizens are awarded rights through these two sources; however, the rights of children are not consistent or clear. From day to day federal, state, and local judiciaries interpret differently the constitutional and legal rights of children. For these reasons, organized efforts must be continuously made to advocate for amendments to the United State Constitution which clearly outline the special and fundamental rights of children. This would force states to recognize the need for comprehensive changes in state codes regarding children, and provide federal, state, and local judiciaries with clearer guidelines in rendering decisions regarding children. It would also provide the base for a national policy on children to guide our institutions in their policy actions toward children and their families.

The most predictable argument by opponents to amending the Constitution will be that this will be detrimental to the stability of the family. The amendment would limit the power of adults, not "only" parents, to make arbitrary decisions concerning the rights of children. It would ensure that children be heard as separate individuals by mandating that decisions made by persons in authority need to be based on the needs, abilities, and responsibilities of all the parties involved.

7. See footnote #8. They are the same.

Following are two lists of children's rights. The first was drafted by the New York State Youth Commission and the second by the General Assembly of the United Nations. Both address the special and fundamental rights of all children. They may be helpful to you in beginning to orient citizens, professionals, and institutions to the concept of children's rights. Hopefully, they will encourage citizen groups to work to have them granted.

Children's Bill of Rights

For each child, regardless of race, color, or creed:

(1) The right to the affection and intelligent guidance of understanding parents.
(2) The right to be raised in a decent home in which he or she is adequately fed, clothed and sheltered.
(3) The right to the benefits of religious guidance and training.
(4) The right to a school program, which in addition to sound academic training, offers maximum opportunity for individual development and preparation for living.
(5) The right to receive constructive discipline for the proper development of good character, conduct and habits.
(6) The right to be secure in his or her community against influences detrimental to proper and wholesome recreation.
(7) The right to individual selection of free and wholesome recreation.
(8) The right to live in a community in which adults practice the belief that the welfare of their children is of primary importance.
(9) The right to receive good adult example.
(10) The right to a job commensurate with his or her ability, training and experience, and protection against physical or moral employment hazards which adversely affect wholesome development.
(11) The right to early diagnosis and treatment of physical handicaps and mental and social maladjustments, at public expense whenever necessary.

Declaration of the Rights of the Child

Principle 1

The child shall enjoy the rights set forth in this Declaration. All children, without any exception whatsoever, shall be entitled to these rights, without distinction or discrimination on account of race, color, sex, language, religion, political or other opinion, national or social origin, property, birth or other status, whether of himself or of his family.

Principle 2

The child shall enjoy special protection, and shall be given opportunities and facilities, by law and by other means, to enable him to develop physically, mentally, spiritually, and socially in a healthy and normal manner and in conditions of freedom and dignity. In the enactment of laws for this purpose the best interests of the child shall be the paramount consideration.

Principle 3

The child shall be entitled from his birth to a name and nationality.

Principle 4

The child shall enjoy the benefits of social security. He shall be entitled to grow and develop in health; to this end special care and protection shall be provided both to him and to his mother, including adequate prenatal and postnatal care. The child shall have the right to adequate nutrition, housing, recreation, and medical services.

Principle 5

The child who is physically, mentally or socially handicapped shall be given the special treatment, education and care required by his particular condition.

Principle 6

The child, for the full and harmonious development of his personality, needs love and understanding. He shall, wherever possible, grow up in the care and under the responsibility of his parents, and in any case in an atmosphere of affection and of moral and material security; a child of tender years shall not, save in exceptional circumstances, be separated from his mother. Society and the public authorities shall have the duty to extend particular care to children without a family and to those without adequate means of support. Payment of state and other assistance toward the maintenance of children of large families is desirable.

Principle 7

The child is entitled to education, which shall be free and compulsory, at least in the elementary stages. He shall be given an education which will promote his general culture, and enable him on a basis of equal opportunity to develop his abilities, his individual judgement, and his sense of moral and social responsibility, and to become a useful member of society. The best interests of the child shall be the guiding principle of those responsible for his education and guidance; that responsibility lies in the first place with his parents. The child shall have full opportunity for play and recreation, which should be directed to the same purposes as education; society and the public authorities shall endeavor to promote the enjoyment of this right.

Principle 8

The child shall in all circumstances be among the first to receive protection and relief.

Principle 9

The child shall be protected against all forms of neglect, cruelty and exploitation. He shall not be the subject of traffic, in any form. The child shall not be admitted to employment before an appropriate minimum age; he shall in no case be caused or permitted to engage in any occupation or employment which would prejudice his health or education, or interfere with his physical, mental or moral development.

Principle 10

The child shall be protected from practices which may foster racial, religious and any other form of discrimination. He shall be brought up in a spirit of understanding, tolerance, friendship among peoples, peace and universal brotherhood and in full consciousness that his energy and talents should be developed to the service of his fellow man.

Adopted unanimously by the General Assembly of the United Nations on November 20, 1959.[8]

It seems to apply today, twenty years later, during and following the International Year of the Child.

8. CHILD ABUSE AND NEGLECT: Prevention and Treatment in Rural Communities. Appalachian Citizens for Children's Rights DHEW Publication No. (OHDS) 78–30154 March 30, 1977.

Chapter 4

The Reporting Laws

(Example: State of California)
- *11110. Record of reports of suspected infliction of physical injury upon minor and arrests for convictions of violation of section 273a.[9]*

The . . . *Department of Justice* shall maintain records of all reports of suspected infliction of physical injury upon a minor by other than accidental means and reports of arrests for, and convictions of, violation of Section 273a. On receipt from a city police department, sheriff or district attorney of a copy of a report of suspected infliction of physical injury upon a minor by other than accidental means received from a physician and surgeon, dentist, resident, intern, chiropractor, religious practitioner, registered nurse employed by a public health agency, school, or school district, director of a county welfare department, or any superintendent of schools of any public or private school system or any principal of a public or private school, the . . . *department* shall transmit to the city police department, sheriff or attorney, information detailing all previous reports of suspected infliction of physical injury upon the same minor or another minor in the same family by other than accidental means and reports of arrests for, and conviction of violation of Section 273a, concerning the same minor or another minor in the same family.

The . . . *department* may adopt rules governing recordkeeping and reporting under Section 11161.5.
(Amended by Stats. 1972, c. 1377, p. 2838, 83.)

- *11161.5 Injuries by other than accidental means, sexual molestation or 273a Injuries to minor; report by physician, teacher, social worker, etc.[10]*

9. California Penal Code Section.
10. ibid.

(a) In any case in which a minor is brought to a physician and surgeon, dentist, intern, podiatrist, chiropractor, *marriage, family or child counselor, psychologist,* or religious practitioner for diagnosis, examination or treatment, or is under his charge or care, or in any case in which a minor is observed by any registered nurse when in the employ of a public health agency, school, or school district and when no physician and surgeon, resident, or intern is present, by any superintendent, any supervisor of child welfare and attendance, or any certificated pupil personnel employee of any public or private school system or any principal of any public or private school, by any teacher of any public or private school, by any licensed day care worker, by an administrator of a public or private summer day camp or child care center, or by a social worker, *by any peace officer, or by any probation officer,* and it appears to the physician and surgeon, dentist, resident, intern, podiatrist, chiropractor, *marriage, family or child counselor, psychologist,* religious practitioner, registered nurse, school superintendent, supervisor of child welfare and attendance, certified pupil personnel employee, school principal, teacher, licensed day care worker, . . . administrator of a public or private summer day camp or child care center, social worker, peace officer, or probation officer, from observation of the minor that the minor has physical injury or injuries which appear to have been inflicted upon him by other than accidental means by any person, that the minor has been sexually molested, or that any injury prohibited by the terms of Section 273a has been inflicted upon the minor, he shall report such fact by telephone and in writing, within 36 hours, to both the local police authority having jurisdiction and to the juvenile probation department; or, in the alternative, either to the county welfare department, or to the county health department. The report shall state, if known, the name of the minor, his whereabouts and the character and extent of the injuries or molestation.

Whenever it is brought to the attention of a director of a county welfare department or health department that a minor has physical injury or injuries which appear to have been inflicted upon him by other than accidental means by any person, that a minor has been sexually molested, or that any injury prohibited by the terms of Section 273a has been inflicted upon a minor, he shall file a report without delay with the local police authority having jurisdiction and . . . *with* the juvenile probation department as provided in this section.

No person shall incur any civil or criminal liability as a result of making any report authorized by this section unless it can be proven that a false report was made and the person knew or should have known that the report was false.

Copies of all written reports received by the local police authority shall be forwarded to the Department of Justice. If the records of the Department of Justice maintained pursuant to Section 11110 or reveal any reports of suspected infliction of physical injury upon, sexual molestation of, or infliction of any injury prohibited by the terms of Section 273a upon, the same minor or any other minor in the same family by other than accidental means, or if the records reveal any arrest or conviction in other localities for a violation of Section 273a inflicted upon the same minor or any other minor in the same family, or if the records reveal any other pertinent information with respect to the same minor or any other minor in the same family, the local reporting agency and the local juvenile probation department shall be immediately notified of the fact.

Reports and other pertinent information received from the department shall be made available to; any licensed physician and surgeon, dentist, resident, intern, podiatrist, chiropractor, *marriage, family, or child counselor, psychologist,* or religious practitioner with regard to his patient or client; any director of a county welfare department, school superintendent, supervisor of child welfare and attendance, certified pupil personnel employee, or school principal having a direct interest in the welfare of the minor; and any probation department, juvenile probation department, or agency offering child protective services.

(b) If the minor is a person specified in Section 300 of the Welfare and Institutions Code and the duty of the probation officer has been transferred to the county welfare department pursuant to Section 576.5 of the Welfare and Institutions Code and the report is made to the local police authority having jurisdiction, then the report required is made to the local police authority having jurisdiction, then the report required by subdivision (a) of this section shall be made to the county welfare department.

Chapter 5

The Criminal Laws

Because child abuse is a crime, regardless of the psychological and social implications involved, it is incumbent upon police officers to be familiar with the statues used in regards to child abuse. Child abusers may be arrested, prosecuted, fined, imprisoned or instructed to take part in treatment programs.

In addition to the penal codes listed below, code sections covering crimes against all persons such as assault with a deadly weapon, battery, manslaughter, murder, disfigurement, incest, sodomy and poisoning may also be applied to child abuse acts.

The California Penal Code Sections pertaining to crimes against children include:

- Physical Assault and Cruel Corporal Punishment:
  SECTION 273d P.C. (Battered Child-Felony); ". . . any person who *willfully inflicts* upon any child any cruel or inhuman corporal punishment or injury resulting in a *traumatic condition,* is guilty of a felony. . . ."
  NOTE: Traumatic condition has been defined as: any wound which results from the application of some external force.
- Physical and Emotional Assault, Emotional Deprivation and Physical Neglect:
  SECTION 273a (1) P.C. (Child Endangering-Felony): "Any person who, under circumstances or conditions *likely to produce* great bodily harm or death, willfully causes or permits any child to suffer, or inflicts thereon unjustifiable physical pain or mental suffering, or having the care or custody of any child, willfully causes or permits the person or health of such child to be injured, or willfully causes or permits such child to be placed in such situation that its person or health is endangered, is punishable by imprisonment. . . ."

SECTION 273a (2) P.C. (Child Endangering-Misdemeanor):
"Any person who, *under circumstances or conditions other than those likely to produce great bodily harm or death,* willfully causes or permits any child to suffer, or inflicts thereon unjustifiable physical pain or mental suffering, or having the care or custody of any child, willfully causes or permits the person or health of such child to be injured, or willfully causes or permits such child to be placed in such situation that its person or health may be endangered, is guilty of a misdemeanor."

NOTE: Section 273a (1) and 273a (2) are the same except "under circumstances or conditions *other* than those likely to produce great bodily harm or death."

SECTION 270 P.C. (Omission to Provide-Misdemeanor): "If a parent of a minor child willfully omits, without lawful excuse, to furnish necessary clothing, food, shelter or medical assistance, or other remedial care for his or her child, he or she is guilty of a misdemeanor. . . ."

SECTION 273g P.C. (Immoral Practicesor Habitual Drunkenness): "Any person who in the presence of any child indulges in any degrading, lewd, immoral or vicious habits or practices in the presence of any child in his care, custody or control, is guilty of a misdemeanor. . . ."

SECTION 272 P.C. (Contributing to Delinquency of Minor-Misdemeanor): "Every person who commits any act or omits the performance of any duty, which act or omission causes or tends to cause or encourage any person under the age of 18 years to come within the provisions of sections 300, 601, or 602 of the Welfare and Institutions code, or which act or omission contributes thereto, or any person who, by any act or omission, or by threats, commands, or persuasion, induces or endeavors to induce any person under the age of 18 years or any ward or dependent child of the juvenile court to fail or refuse to conform to a lawful order of the juvenile court, or to do or to perform any act or to follow any course of conduct or to so live as would cause or manifestly tend to cause any such person to become or to remain a person within the provisions of Section 300, 601 or 602 W.I.C., is guilty of a misdemeanor. . . ."

NOTE: Section 272 P.C. is all encompassing, and should be considered when difficulty arises in filing section 273 P.C. or in simple neglect cases when documentation is available, i.e., previous police contacts.

- Sexual Exploitation:[11]

  SECTION 288 P.C. (Lewd or Lascivious Acts-Felony): "Any person who shall willfully and lewdly commit any lewd or lascivious act including any of the acts constituting other crimes provided for in part one of this code upon or with the body, or any part or member thereof, of a child under the age of fourteen years, with the intent of arousing, appealing to, or gratifying the lust or passions or sexual desires of such person or of such child, shall be guilty of a felony. . . ."

  SECTION 261.5 P.C. (Unlawful Sexual Intercourse): "Unlawful sexual Intercourse is an act of sexual intercourse accomplished with a female not the wife of the perpetrator, where the female is under the age of 18 years." (Also known as statutory rape.)

- **CALIFORNIA WELFARE AND INSTITUTIONS CODE:** Sections pertaining to crimes against children. The WIC sections are important for the officer to know as they provide the reason(s) and authority for taking a minor/victim into protective custody and investigating the circumstances.

  1. Legal Authority for Arrest (Protective Custody)

     SECTION 305 W.I.C.: . . . "A peace officer may, without a warrant, take into temporary custody a minor under 18 when he has reasonable cause to believe that such minor is a person described in Section 300 W.I.C."

     SECTION 300 W.I.C.: "Any person under the age of 18 years who comes within any of the following descriptions is within the jurisdiction of the juvenile court which may adjudge such person to be a dependent child of the court."

     SECTION 300 (a) W.I.C.: Who is in need of proper and effective parental care or control and has no parent or guardian, or has no parent or guardian willing to exercise or capable of exercising such care or control, or has no parent or guardian actually exercising such care or control.

     SECTION 300 (b) W.I.C.: Who is destitute, or who is not provided with the necessities of life, or who is not provided with a home or suitable place of abode.

     SECTION 300 (d) W.I.C.: Whose home is an unfit place for him by reason of neglect, cruelty, depravity or physical abuse of either of his parents, or of his guardian or other person in whose custody or care he is."

11. Refer to 311 P.C. regarding Pornography.

Chapter 6

Recognition and Response

The key to recognition and response is simply a matter of "knowing what to look for." Becoming familiar with what a child doesn't say as opposed to voluntary responses by the child. A good rule of thumb is, "not telling the truth, may be telling all," in the case of the battering or abusing parent, guardian, etc. A child may not cooperate for a myriad of reasons, but an adults story-telling may in fact be just what you are looking for.

Beyond general interviewing and interrogation techniques, the categorical sequencing of injuries may be helpful in recognition. The following photos in the color insert are included to offer vivid indication of. I. Whipping, II. Bruises, III. Burns, and IV. Central Nervous System (brain injury). It should be noted that not all injuries are as easily detected as those shown here, particularly sexual assault injuries.

Chapter 7

Guidelines for Handling "Suspected" Child Abuse

When a patrol officer is assigned to take a report in a suspected child abuse/neglect situation, the decisions the officer makes and the completeness of the information collected, may save the life of the child. This is also true if the first public officer involved is a probation officer or public welfare officer.

The danger facing minor victims of abuse/neglect cannot be over-emphasized. One expert has stated that in 25 percent of the cases where the battered child is returned to it's parents, that child will later be permanently disabled or killed by those parents. That is why we cannot tolerate a case which is lost due to improper reporting, lack of appropriate police action, bad prosecution or poor social casework.

Abuse and neglect cases should be handled as though they were major cases. That is, the evidence should be gathered in a sophisticated manner and with uncanny thoroughness. This can be of utmost importance where there are no witnesses to testify, which happens frequently.

The following steps and procedures are guidelines to be followed by preliminary investigating officers. The concern here is that an investigation that appears "seemingly routine" could lull you into ignoring or omitting needed procedures that, had the steps been taken, would have allowed for an intelligent case disposition. These procedures are provided to continuously remind and reenforce the needed procedures.

Determinants for Taking
Minors into Protective Custody

It is the responsibility of the police officer to determine whether a child should be removed from his home or parental custody and placed in police protective custody. The guidelines for taking minors into protective custody should be based on the safety and welfare of the minor.

33

If leaving the minor(s) in the home could cause further physical or mental suffering, they shall be taken into protective custody.*

It is your responsibility as the preliminary investigating officer to, as in all cases, exercise common sense and to make a diligent effort to be as complete in your investigation as possible. With the appropriate information in a timely manner, the proper decision can be made to insure the protection of the minor(s). In many cases, one chance to be seen and saved may be the only chance a child may have.

Standard rule of practice—"When in doubt, take the kid. It's easier to say 'I'm sorry,' than be sorry."

Preliminary Investigation Report
or Case Report

All cases, whether referred to and handled by another agency or not, require a preliminary investigation report of some type with all medical report forms attached. Thoroughness here cannot be over-emphasized.

As with any investigation report, it is most important that you include all pertinent information and relay a *COMPLETE* account of the circumstances as you have ascertained them.

Following is a guideline for information which must be included on the report:

1. Minor(s) full name; address; date of birth; physical description; phone number.
2. Parent's full name; address; phone number; date of birth; driver's license number (if possible). (Guardian if applicable.)
3. Suspect (if any) full name; address; phone number; date of birth (if possible); physical description.
4. If person(s) bringing minor(s) to hospital is different from the parents—acquire his/her name; address; phone number; and any other identifying information possible on such person(s).
5. Doctor's full name; address; phone number.
6. Assigned hospital social worker's full name; address; phone number.
7. Date and time report was made.

*Use Section 305. W & I Code in California.

8. Date, time and *place of occurrence.*

> NOTE: It must be stressed that it is important to document *where* the incident occurred. Residence address and occurrence of incident often may differ. If and when abuse is established, the case is turned over to the municipality of *where* the incident occurred.

9. Complete account of circumstances, noting particularly mental & emotional state of child.
10. Agency handling the case (if applicable).
11. Final disposition of minor(s). Include welfare caseworker's name.
12. Time, date of contacting and information received from Child Abuse Reporting Center, Department of Justice, State of California. It is here as required by 11110. P.C., in California, that all reports are centrally indexed.

- **RESPONSE—HOSPITAL-INITIATED CALL**
  When responding to a call from a hospital, you should:
- **INTERVIEW:** Interview the physician and *all* hospital staff who can provide information concerning the circumstances surrounding the minor's injuries. A social worker is automatically assigned by the hospital to interview the family. *Be sure* to interview the social worker as part of the hospital staff involved. Inquire from the medical staff:
  a. How do the medical personnel believe the injuries occurred?
  b. Is the parents/caretakers explanation of how the injury occurred consistent with medical evidence?
  c. What statements, if any, were made by the mother, father, step-parent, etc., to medical personnel?
  d. Is there evidence of old injuries?
  e. Is there evidence of sexual abuse?
  f. What medical records, reports, etc., exist?
  g. What x-rays exist?
  h. Always consider use of dermatologists, pediatricians, and odontologists as experts.
- **OBTAIN MEDICAL RECORDS:** Be sure to acquire from the attending physician a completed medical report-suspected child abuse form and copies of any other medical treatment forms they are willing to release. (Please refer to examples herein.) If another agency handles the case, they will take the original and you must get a copy.

It is important to be aware that court appearances by professional medical personnel may be avoided if the mandated reporting forms are filled out legibly and completely. Additionally, the form is a business record exception to the hearsay rule and can be admitted in evidence without necessarily requiring the doctor's appearance.

- **DETERMINATION OF INCIDENT OF ABUSE:** The preliminary investigation officer, with the assistance of the hospital staff, must determine by comparing the medical diagnosis to the story/explanation that was given by whomever brought the minor(s) to the hospital, if there is evidence of child abuse and/or neglect.
- **PHOTOGRAPHS:** If there are obvious signs of physical abuse such as bruises, welts, cuts or abrasions, color photographs should be taken as soon as possible. A complete, detailed written description of what was observed should accompany any photos taken. These photos will be released to the agency handling the case. Black and white photos do not depict injury as well as colored photographs.
- **DISPOSITION OF MINOR(S):** Before leaving the hospital, find out what the final disposition of the minor(s) is to be, i.e., stay at the hospital, and/or taken into protective custody under section 300 W.I.C., or released to parental care.

Suspected abuse investigations can lead to two types of court action. First, a dependency petition may be filed in juvenile court to remove the minor from the custody of the parents/caretakers; second, a criminal complaint may be filed against the responsible parties. In any given case, either or both of these actions may occur.

It is important for the patrol officer to recognize this, because rules of evidence and the burdens of proof differ in each proceedings, and evidence which is not admissible in a criminal trial may well be admissible in the juvenile court case.

This distinction results from the intent of the juvenile proceedings, which is *to protect the minor*. The difference in burden of proof refers to the fact that the criminal case must, of course, be proven beyond a reasonable doubt, while the dependency petition in juvenile court needs only to be proven by a preponderence of the evidence.

When an officer is assigned a suspected child abuse call, he should:

- **INTERVIEW:** Interview all parties including complainants, parents/caretakers, minor(s) and whoever else is at the scene. Obtain details regarding the incident:
  - a. What did occur?
  - b. How did it occur?
  - c. Who caused it?
  - d. What action was taken by those present when incident was discovered?
  - e. How soon after the incident occurred or was discovered, did those present take action?
  - f. Photographs of scene as they substantiate the interview.

    If at such time the interview becomes accusatory, the exclusionary rule applies, therefore evidence is admissible only if rules regarding search and seizure have been followed. Only "unfit home" cases are the exception.

    If the objective of interview is only for the purpose of dependency action, the exclusionary rule does not apply.
- **OBSERVATION:** Observe the physical condition of the child. Consider the attitude of the parents/caretakers towards the child. Consider the general environment including living conditions and health and moral hazards.
- **EVALUATION:** Evaluate evidence of the suspected abuse/neglect to determine if it may continue and endanger the safety of the child.

    If you determine removal and/or further police involvement is NOT necessary, record the incident fully and file your investigation report at the station.
- **EVIDENCE:** Collect, preserve and book all possible items of evidential value in the abuse case, i.e. clothing, weapons, broken furniture, kitchen utensils, cigarettes used to inflict burns, etc.
- **PHOTOGRAPHS:** Photos should be taken of any situation that might indicate abuse and neglect. A written description of what was observed should accompany any photos taken. ALL PHOTOS SHOULD BE IN COLOR, 8″ × 10″ in size.
- **REMOVAL:** If warranted, remove the minor(s) from the home as soon as possible.

- **NOTES:** Take extensive notes—times, observations, statements—remember photographs sometimes do not turn out.
- **REMINDERS:** When responding to the scene of suspected child abuse/neglect, or when suspected abuse/neglect is observed at the scene, the officer must remember that his immediate concern and responsibility is for the safety and welfare of the minor(s).

Chapter 8

Guidelines for Schools: Recognition and Response

Penal Code Section 11161.5 requires that any nurse, certified pupil personnel employee, supervisor of child welfare and attendance, principal, teacher, licensed day care worker shall report incidents of abuse of minors to a legally responsible authority. Abuse includes circumstances or conditions likely to produce great bodily harm, unjustifiable physical pain or mental suffering, the permission of such situation that a child's person or health is endangered (11161.5, Section 273 a).

Schools are therefore charged by the law to act to protect the children in their care from family or community abuse or neglect. This requires observation of children, awareness of home conditions and a structure for carrying out the direction of the law. The school can be a prime resource for protection of the children when procedures for doing so are available. The following areas of responsibility belong within the school's authority.

Reporting

Because there is a need for judgment in determining a reportable incident, a particular certificated person can be designated as the authority to make the determination. *The law states that the appearance of neglect or abuse is sufficient to support a report.* The law states that the permission of conditions that endanger a child is a violation. An immediate telephone report is made to both local police authority and the County Child Protective Service. A written report is made within 36 hours.

A school district may devise its own report form which insures consistency and accountability in the reporting service. School personnel need to understand that they are protected by law from civil or criminal liability as a result of making a report.

Because of differences in responsibilities, judgments need to be made about receiving agencies. Actual injuries, sexual abuse, acute neglect, serious threats against children, situations of danger to a child's health or welfare are referred to police and to Child Protective Service. These agencies have the authority to take immediate protective action. Pervasive but less acute mistreatment is referred to the Child Protective Service or a public health nurse. These agencies are counseling services.

The definition of a reportable instance is not ever a simple matter and some acceptance of the cultural standards of a community may be involved. In general, these may be considered to be reportable situations:

1. Any bruises (mild or severe), burns or injuries that are not clearly accidental and compatible with the causal event as described by child and/or parent.
2. All reports of sexual mistreatment.
3. Reports by small children of being left unattended for extended periods.
4. Reports by children under 14 years of age being left alone all night.
5. Children who are persistently and significantly dirtier than the community standard.
6. Unmet health needs of a serious nature.
7. Knowledge of cruel or unusual punishment or expectations.
8. Reports by a child of seriously aberrant behavior of a parent. This includes behaviors that represent a physical or emotional danger to the child (drinking, irrational acts or beliefs).
9. Statements by parents of intent to do bodily harm to their children.

It is helpful to school personnel to keep in mind that the school is not the investigating agency. The school refers for investigation and cooperates with investigation. The legally responsible agency decides the abuse charge.

Detection

Observations of children's behavior may help teachers to determine which children need help. These characteristics in a child may be signals strongly suggestive of an urgent need for evaluation and assistance.

1. Persistent unverified absences from school.
2. Fear of adults.
3. Timidity and withdrawal.
4. Anxiety about authority and fearfulness about expectations.
5. Thirst for affection and attention.
6. Worry about parents.
7. Inappropriate and frequent anger.
8. Behavior that provokes punishment.

Some children who have been abused react by anxiously watching adult expectations and straining to anticipate and conform. Others provoke adults to anger and respond with hostility to relieve the rage within. Either extreme should serve as a clue to the school personnel that the situation the child comes from may be hazardous.

Observation of the parent is another source of information for the school. Extremes of these behaviors should alert teachers to the potential of mistreatment:

1. Unsympathetic and frequent criticism of the child.
2. Anger and defensiveness about school reports.
3. Inappropriate expectations of children in behavior or achievement.
4. Demands that the school use corporal punishment as a control method.
5. Relating of a personal history of deprivation or abuse.
6. Dramatically self-centered and immature behavior.
7. Temper and impulsivity.
8. Depressive moods.
9. Alienation from friends and extended family. An important question to ask a potentially abusive parent is, "Is there anyone to help you?"

Early preventive referrals to schools and community counseling and treatment services may be made when these characteristics are observed in child or parent.

Contact with Parents

School personnel are important to the potentially abusive family because of the school's traditional role of evaluation of a child's achievement and behavior and because of the authority accorded the school in the area of child supervision. In their book, *Helping the Battered Child and His Family,* Pollock and Steele say of abusive parents:

"There is no specific psychiatric diagnosis which encompasses
the personalities and behavior of all of them. They share,
however, a common pattern of parent-child relationships or style
of child rearing characterized by a high demand for the child to
perform so as to gratify the parents, and by use of severe
physical punishment to ensure the child's proper behavior.
Abusive parents also show an unusually high vulnerability to
criticism, disinterest or abandonment by the spouse or other
important person, or anything that lowers their already
inadequate self-esteem. Such events create a crisis of unmet
needs in the parents, who then turns to the child with
exaggerated demands for gratification. The child is often unable
to meet such parental expectations and is punished excessively."

Certainly the school's contact with a family about a child can trigger abuse. Schools need to be aware of safe ways of dealing with families they judge to be high risk. Following are some considerations for these families:

1. In some situations, handling as much as possible at school without involving the parents may be a genuinely helpful process. The home crisis is avoided, the child learns that behavior is dealt with in another way at school. Perceptive children understand efforts to protect them.

2. When a conference is needed, the parent's extreme sensitivity to criticism and his tendency to seek gratification through his child must be recognized. Statements about misbehavior or learning difficulties can be worded as problems to be worked on together. Parents help is elicited in terms of its importance to school and child. Specific suggestions of what the parent is expected to do to support the school can be made.

3. The referral of high risk parents to agency help is often determined by the practicalities of the situation. What are the parents willing to do? Are they willing to work on their problem voluntarily with a private practitioner or agency? If not,

is there a situation that is clear-cut enough to call on a legally responsible service? When a report to another agency must be made, it must be explained to the family clearly in terms of the law. This is no time for censure or questions or apology. "This is the law and we followed it." Present the receiving agency in as helpful a way as possible.

4. If neither above alternative is possible, the school must help because it is all there is. In his book, *Violence Against Children,* David Gil's first recommendation is to change a culturally determined permissive attitude toward the use of physical force in child discipline. This is something that the school can do, by example and by counsel. A parent's attitude can be assessed and directed toward a humane and reasonable method of child care by a teacher, nurse, counselor or principal. The school staff bears an inherent community authority in regard to children.

5. Counseling abusive parents is a sensitive process and school personnel cannot be expected to carry large responsibilities in this area. However, they do have constant contacts with the parents and need to know how to handle them. The staff person must strive to be nonjudgmental. He must be able to appreciate the parent's own needs and feelings. He can offer the parent practical, planned suggestions to meet the specific situations that give this parent trouble.

6. Hardest for teachers are situations in which parents meet them with persistent anger and hostility. Whenever possible, these situations should be handled by school counseling and casework services with special skills in handling hostile situations. The teacher and child are free to relate without the interference of the teacher's anxiety or resentment or the child's humiliation over an unfortunate teacher-parent confrontation.

Contacts with Children

An understanding and alert school staff can extend to child abuse victims the extra patience and affection that the children need. They can give children day by day living experiences with reasonable rules and expectations and consistent acceptance in spite of mistakes and even provocation. It is a different kind of life experience than is offered at home. Some particular experiences that a child can have at school are these:

1. An abused child can be encouraged in a child-adult relationship that may be corrective and healing. He can learn about rational discipline and reasonable life patterns.
2. An abused child can be helped to behave in socially acceptable ways to protect himself and minimize abuse.
3. A child from a high-risk home can receive support and counseling at school that helps him cope with hard situations that cannot be changed.
4. When reports are made to agencies, the school staff can be supportive of the children going through the anxious ordeal of investigation. On occasions, school staff have accompanied children to receiving homes, hospitals, juvenile facilities and court hearings.
5. A school can give a child permission, support and channels to ask for protection for himself and his siblings.

Contacts with Agencies

The school can assist other agencies by being observant and making factual, clear and unbiased reports. A school can be the source of a professional evaluation of the situation which should be above the community's prejudice. A school can document a report with dates, incidents, specifics.

The referral that has to be made on the child's work may be the hardest of all because it sometimes makes the school staff feel that they have betrayed the child. All referrals need careful thoughtful agency cooperation. They need especially sensitive planning and careful handling.

Schools can assist agencies by presenting agency services in constructive terms to families. Schools can support the family "on probation" through the trials of bringing about different family living patterns. Teachers can diminish the stigma of such legal interferences in the family's life by acceptance and support.

Schools can help most by the careful daily observations of children from high-risk homes and by coordination of efforts with other supervising professionals. Alerting the social worker that there is a time of stress in the family may alleviate this problem. Reporting a minor bruise may prevent a major one. No other agency has the daily contact with children that gives the opportunity to identify the deteriorating problem before it explodes.

Chapter 9

Record-Keeping

Construct a legally acceptable record of facts for any potential legal proceeding. This of course, would begin with initial contact. A police officer would rely on his field notes, radio log, and initial report. A probation officer might become involved in a case at the point of intake, or possibly as a member of the child abuse team if one exists. A physician would become involved during the initial medical exam, and subsequent examinations, including laboratory tests and possibly contact with a victim who was hospitalized. Appropriate information from the medical social worker may also prove useful. Don't forget the family dentist, as a forensic odonlogist may call upon his records.

Often times parents, guardians, etc., appear open and receptive to intervention. Remember, court action may ensue so be sure dates, times, names and other points of exploration and investigation are kept. Non-judicial resolution is what most people are working toward, but this does not obviate the necessity for contingency planning for eventual court use. All too often, petitions are filed by the District Attorney's office on the basis of the child protection report system and initial police reports. No filing will occur if reports are haphazardly constructed or insufficient in terms of evidentiary considerations.

Often, identifying conditions by use of a check sheet can be not only helpful, but easier than exhaustive reports. A check-off sheet could embrace in any form, the outline herein:

1. Type of Abuse
   A. Physical
   B. Sexual
   C. Neglect
      1. Child given excessive responsibility.
      2. Child given excessive physical work.
      3. Child required to steal, beg, panhandle, or solicit.
      4. Malnourished
      5. In need of health care

6. Unbathed
7. Fails to attend school
8. Beyond care due to no supervision
9. Unattended
10. Abandoned
11. Denied affection partially
12. Denied affection totally
13. Improperly clothed
14. Poor or inadequate housing
15. Poor or inadequate diet
16. Injury—visible
17. Injury—not visible
18. Medical care—emergency

II. Type of Parents or Guardian
   A. Two Parent Family
   B. Single Parent Family
   C. Man assuming role of spouse (Mars Man)
   D. Live-in Child Care
   E. Foster Care
   F. Conditions
      1. Natural
      2. Step
      3. Foster
      4. Relatives
      5. Marital discord
      6. Divorced or separated
      7. Alcohol problem
      8. Drug (illicit) problem
      9. Other children *(List number of others)*

III. Environment
   A. Criminal
   B. Illicit sex
   C. Hours prescribed for eating, sleeping, etc. (Yes or No).
   D. Acceptable learning/value system.

IV. Financial Support System
   A. *(List those working)*
   B. Insurance, i.e., Unemployment Compensation or Disability.
   C. Welfare, i.e., AFDC (Aid to Families with Dependent Children).
   D. Pension
   E. Other

V. Other Public Agency Involvement
   A. Probation
   B. Parole
   C. Department of Public Welfare
   D. Hospital
VI. General Information
   A. Neighborhood Complaints
      1. Complaints from neighbors
      2. Complaints from relatives
      3. Complaints from school authorities
      4. Complaints from other public agencies
   B. Contact with Private Social Service Agency
   C. Other with knowledge of family.

In the process of answering the concerns developed in the outline, it is readily apparent that much of this information is not only important for use in court, but very simply, extremely helpful in working with the family unit outside the judicial system. Additional information, no doubt, will become available as the case is further developed.

The greater emphasis on rules of evidence and court conduct in cases where child victims are involved has precipitated new performance standards. Regardless of the profession, those involved in crimes against children cases find a tremendous emphasis on strict application to the common rules of evidence. Developing a record of activities then, to support ones' actions, is highly recommended.

Once recognition has occurred, the response phase is initiated. Response most certainly must begin with reporting; as well as immediate medical assistance should it be needed. Law enforcement agencies would in most cases file a crime report, but often, the police agency within its juvenile division, may use diversion or specialized response and reporting. In many cases, a child abuse investigator, may contact the County Probation Department, Department of Public Welfare, and possibly a medical case worker. This team approach has proven to be very successful. There are however, general forms which are required by local agency policy, in addition to the State law requirements. Examples of the possible forms are included in order to demonstrate a possible model which may be used—or standard procedure forms.

Included are: Typical Crime Report,—Probation Form No. 516,—Medical Report—Suspected Sexual Assault Form 923,—Childrens Hospital and Health Center Sex Abuse History and Physical Exam Check off Sheet,—Childrens Hospital and Health Center Sexual Abuse Laboratory Check-off and Order Sheets #1 and #2.

The completion of the various forms is not busy work. Forms cannot be underestimated. They provide valuable information on medical treatment administered, all personnel from the various agencies which are involved, initial reports, follow-up investigations, and are useful to the courts for evidentiary consideration. In addition, social service agencies in some cases can begin to paint a portrait of the entire situation, and with the involvement of the parties involved, offer post-incident, post-judicial assistance.

CRIME/INCIDENT REPORT

CRIME

VICTIM INDEMNIFICATION REQ. ☐ YES ☐ NO

DISPATCHED ☐ / VIA TELEPHONE ☐ / OFF. INITIATED ☐

TYPE OF CRIME OR INCIDENT (ONE INCIDENT ONLY)   MONTH / DAY / YEAR / DAY OF WEEK / TIME /

LOCATION OF INCIDENT (OR ADDRESS)   FIRM NAME (IF COMMERCIAL)

VICTIM — WITNESS

VICTIM'S NAME (LAST, FIRST, MIDDLE) | RESIDENCE ADDRESS | CITY | STATE | RESIDENCE PHONE | RACE | SEX

EMPLOYER, SCHOOL, DUTY STATION | WORK HOURS | BUSINESS OR MILITARY ADDRESS | BUSINESS PHONE | DATE OF BIRTH

V W RP DC   NAME (LAST, FIRST, MIDDLE) | RESIDENCE ADDRESS | CITY | STATE | RESIDENCE PHONE | RACE | SEX

EMPLOYER, SCHOOL, DUTY STATION | WORK HOURS | BUSINESS OR MILITARY ADDRESS | BUSINESS PHONE | DATE OF BIRTH

V W RP DC   NAME (LAST, FIRST, MIDDLE) | RESIDENCE ADDRESS | CITY | STATE | RESIDENCE PHONE | RACE | SEX

EMPLOYER, SCHOOL, DUTY STATION | WORK HOURS | BUSINESS OR MILITARY ADDRESS | BUSINESS PHONE | ADD'L. PERSONS LISTED?

PLACE OF ATTACK: ☐ STRUCTURE ☐ STREET/ALLEY ☐ OTHER _____ ☐ VEHICLE ☐ LOT/PARK/YARD _____

DESCRIPTION OF SURROUNDING AREA: 1 ☐ RESIDENTIAL 3 ☐ INDUSTRIAL/MFG. 5 ☐ INSTITUTIONAL 7 ☐ OTHER
2 ☐ BUSINESS 4 ☐ RECREATIONAL 6 ☐ OPEN SPACE

AGE OF STRUCTURE:

LIST TOOLS, WEAPONS, OR FORCE USED, AND HOW USED

M.O. INFORMATION

TYPE OF STRUCTURE
0 ☐ N/A

Non-Residential
1 ☐ Convenience
2 ☐ Drug/Medical
3 ☐ Fast Food
4 ☐ Financial
5 ☐ Mfg./Construc.
6 ☐ Other Retail
7 ☐ Public Bldg.
8 ☐ Restaurant/Bar
9 ☐ Services
10 ☐ Transportation
11 ☐ Wholesale
12 ☐ Other

Residential
1 ☐ Apt./Condo
2 ☐ Duplex/Townhs
3 ☐ Hotel/Motel
4 ☐ Mobile/Camper
5 ☐ Sgl. Detached
6 ☐ Other

Target(s)
1 ☐ Attic
2 ☐ Basement
3 ☐ Bathroom
4 ☐ Bedroom
5 ☐ Den
6 ☐ Family Room
7 ☐ Garage/Carport
8 ☐ Kitchen
9 ☐ Living Room
10 ☐ Person
11 ☐ Storage Area
12 ☐ Other

Target(s)
1 ☐ Cash Reg./Dwr.
2 ☐ Display Items
3 ☐ Person
4 ☐ Safe/Box
5 ☐ Sales Area
6 ☐ Vending Mach.
7 ☐ Other

POINT OF ENTRY
1 ☐ N/A
2 ☐ Unknown
3 ☐ Front
4 ☐ Garage
5 ☐ Rear
6 ☐ Side
7 ☐ Ground Level
8 ☐ Upper Level
9 ☐ Door
10 ☐ Duct/Vent
11 ☐ Roof/Floor
12 ☐ Trunk/Hood
13 ☐ Wall
14 ☐ Window
15 ☐ Other

EXIT:

POE VISIBLE FROM
1 ☐ Adj. Structure
2 ☐ Alley
3 ☐ Street
4 ☐ Not Visible

SECURITY USED
1 ☐ N/A
2 ☐ Alarm
3 ☐ Bars/Grate
4 ☐ Dog
5 ☐ Ext. Lights
6 ☐ Guard/Watchman
7 ☐ Int. Lights
8 ☐ Locked - Doors
9 ☐ Locked - Windows
10 ☐ Neighbor, Watch
11 ☐ Operation ID
12 ☐ Photo/Camera
13 ☐ Security Fence
14 ☐ Other

TYPE LOCK DEFEATED
1 ☐ N/A
2 ☐ Chain/Bolt
3 ☐ Deadbolt
4 ☐ Padlock
5 ☐ Springlatch
6 ☐ Springlatch D.B.L.
7 ☐ Other

SUSPECT PRETENDED TO BE
1 ☐ N/A
2 ☐ Conducting Survey
3 ☐ Customer/Client
4 ☐ Delivery Person
5 ☐ Disabled Motorist
6 ☐ Drunk
7 ☐ Employee/Employer
8 ☐ Friend/Relative
9 ☐ Ill/Injured
10 ☐ Need Phone
11 ☐ Police/Law
12 ☐ Renter
13 ☐ Repairman
14 ☐ Salesperson
15 ☐ Seeking Assist.
16 ☐ Seeking Directions
17 ☐ Seeking Someone
18 ☐ Selling Illegal Goods/Services
19 ☐ Soliciting Funds
20 ☐ Other

SUSPECT ACTIONS
0 ☐ Unknown
1 ☐ Bound Victim
2 ☐ Blindfolded Victim
3 ☐ Child Molest
4 ☐ Defecated
5 ☐ Demanded Cash
6 ☐ Demanded Jewelry
7 ☐ Disabled Phone
8 ☐ Ate/Drank on Premises
9 ☐ Forced Victim to Move
10 ☐ Hideout Technique
11 ☐ Inflicted Injury
12 ☐ Other Sex Acts
13 ☐ Prepared Exit
14 ☐ Ransacked
15 ☐ Raped
16 ☐ Smoked on Prem.
17 ☐ Took Only Concealables
18 ☐ Took Only Money
19 ☐ Took Only Tools
20 ☐ Took Only TV/Stero
21 ☐ Took Victim's Vehicle
22 ☐ Threatened Retaliation
23 ☐ Used Lookout
24 ☐ Used Demand Note
25 ☐ Used Force to Gain Entry
26 ☐ Used Matches for Light
27 ☐ Used Stolen Vehicle
28 ☐ Used Victim's Tools
29 ☐ Vandalized
30 ☐ Vehicle Needed to Remove Property
31 ☐ Was Neat
32 ☐ Other

FURTHER DESCRIPTION (INCLUDE TRADEMARKS OR UNUSUAL ACTS OF SUSPECT)

EVID.

EVIDENCE OBTAINED: 1 ☐ FINGERPRINTS 4 ☐ VEHICLE 7 ☐ STAINS 2 ☐ OTHER PRINTS 5 ☐ PHOTOS 8 ☐ BLOOD/SEMEN 0 ☐ NONE 3 ☐ WEAPON/TOOLS 6 ☐ HAIR 9 ☐ OTHER

DISPOSITION OF EVIDENCE   TAG NOS.

PROPERTY

ITEM NO.	ARTICLE NAME	QTY	IDENTIFICATION NUMBERS	BRAND, MAKE, OR MANUFACTURER	MODEL NAME AND MODEL NUMBERS	MISCELLANEOUS DESCRIPTION	VALUE

ADDITIONAL PROPERTY LISTED ☐ YES ☐ NO

CASH NOTES $ PURS $ OFFICE EQUIP. $ FIREARMS $ CONSUMABLE GOODS $ MISC. $

JEWELRY, PREC. MET. $ CLOTHING $ TV, RADIOS, CAMERAS $ HOUSEHOLD GOODS $ LIVESTOCK $ TOTAL: $

BIKE ONLY | FRAME NO. | ☐ BOYS ☐ GIRLS ☐ MO-PED | WHEEL SIZE ____ INCH | FRAME COLOR | TRIM COLOR | LICENSE NO. | BRAKE TYPE | AGE | NO. OF GEARS | HEADLIGHT ☐ YES ☐ NO | BASKET ☐ YES ☐ NO

ADMINISTRATIVE

I AM AWARE THAT IT IS UNLAWFUL TO MAKE A FALSE REPORT TO A POLICE OFFICER. I AFFIRM THAT THE ABOVE INFORMATION IS TRUE TO THE BEST OF MY KNOWLEDGE.

VICTIM'S SIGNATURE:

RELATED REPORTS ☐ NO ☐ YES   TYPE: | VICTIM TO CONTACT DETECTIVES: ☐ NO ☐ YES ←(PERSONS) ☐ YES ←(PROPERTY) | DATE/TIME | DIVISION | DETECTIVE(S) ASSIGNED!

REPORTING OFFICER | DIVISION | I.D. # | APPROVED BY: | SUSPECT IN CUSTODY: ☐ YES ☐ ADULT ☐ JUVENILE ☐ NO - PROBABLY IS [A] [J] [T]

DATE AND TIME OF REPORT   MO.   DAY   YEAR   TIME: | CRIME TYPE | BEAT | DISTRICT

SUSPECT #1 (LAST, FIRST, MIDDLE)			NICKNAME/AKA	RACE	SEX	AGE	HT.	WT.	BUILD	HAIR	EYES	DOB
SUSPECT'S ADDRESS			CLOTHING DESCRIPTION									ARRESTED 1 ☐ YES 2 ☐ NO
SUSPECT #2 (LAST, FIRST, MIDDLE)			NICKNAME/AKA	RACE	SEX	AGE	HT.	WT.	BUILD	HAIR	EYES	DOB
SUSPECT'S ADDRESS			CLOTHING DESCRIPTION									ARRESTED 1 ☐ YES 2 ☐ NO

SUSPECT(S)

HAIR LGTH/TYPE	HAIR STYLE	FACIAL HAIR	COMPLEXION	GENERAL APPEARANCE	DEMEANOR	SPEECH	VOICE
1 2 SUSPECT	1 2 SUSPECT	1 2 SUSPECT	1 2 SUSPECT	1 2 SUSPECT	1 2 SUSPECT	1 2 SUSPECT	1 2 SUSPECT
0 ☐☐ Unknown	0 ☐☐ Unknown	0 ☐☐ Unknown	0 ☐☐ Unknown	0 ☐☐ Unknown	0 ☐☐ Unknown	0 ☐☐ Unknown	0 ☐☐ Unknown
1 ☐☐ Bald	1 ☐☐ Afro/Nat	1 ☐☐ Clean Shave	1 ☐☐ Acne	1 ☐☐ Conservative	1 ☐☐ Angry	1 ☐☐ Accent	1 ☐☐ Disguised
2 ☐☐ Collar	2 ☐☐ Braided	2 ☐☐ Full Beard	2 ☐☐ Dark	2 ☐☐ Dirty	2 ☐☐ Apologetic	2 ☐☐ Lisps	2 ☐☐ High Pitch
3 ☐☐ Long	3 ☐☐ Bushy	3 ☐☐ Fu Manchu	3 ☐☐ Freckled	3 ☐☐ Disguise	3 ☐☐ Calm	3 ☐☐ Mumbles	3 ☐☐ Loud
4 ☐☐ Shoulder	4 ☐☐ Greasy	4 ☐☐ Goatee	4 ☐☐ Light	4 ☐☐ Flashy	4 ☐☐ Disorganized	4 ☐☐ Offensive	4 ☐☐ Low Pitch
5 ☐☐ Short	5 ☐☐ Military	5 ☐☐ Lower Lip	5 ☐☐ Medium	5 ☐☐ Good-Looking	5 ☐☐ Irrational	5 ☐☐ Quiet	5 ☐☐ Medium
6 ☐☐ Coarse	6 ☐☐ Ponytail	6 ☐☐ Mustache	6 ☐☐ Pale	6 ☐☐ Military	6 ☐☐ Nervous	6 ☐☐ Rapid	6 ☐☐ Monotone
7 ☐☐ Fine	7 ☐☐ Processed	7 ☐☐ None/Fuzz	7 ☐☐ Pocked	7 ☐☐ Unkempt	7 ☐☐ Polite	7 ☐☐ Slow	7 ☐☐ Nasal
8 ☐☐ Thick	8 ☐☐ Straight	8 ☐☐ Sideburns	8 ☐☐ Ruddy	8 ☐☐ Unusual Odor	8 ☐☐ Professional	8 ☐☐ Stutters	8 ☐☐ Pleasant
9 ☐☐ Thinning	9 ☐☐ Wavy/Curly	9 ☐☐ Unshaven	9 ☐☐ Sallow	9 ☐☐ Well Groomed	9 ☐☐ Stupor	9 ☐☐ Talkative	9 ☐☐ Raspy
9 ☐☐ Wiry	10 ☐☐ Wig	10 ☐☐ Van Dyke	10 ☐☐ Tanned	10 ☐☐ Other	10 ☐☐ Violent	10 ☐☐ Other	10 ☐☐ Soft
9 ☐☐ Other	11 ☐☐ Other	11 ☐☐ Other	11 ☐☐ Other		11 ☐☐ Other		11 ☐☐ Other

FURTHER SUSPECT DESCRIPTION (I.E., GLASSES, TATOOS, TEETH, BIRTHMARKS, JEWELRY, SCARS, MANNERISMS, ETC.)

ADDITIONAL SUSPECTS LISTED? 1 ☐ YES 2 ☐ NO

VEHICLE	YEAR	MAKE	MODEL	COLOR/COLOR	BODY STYLE	LICENSE NO.	STATE

ADDITIONAL VEHICLE IDENTIFIERS (DAMAGE, CHROME WHEELS, ETC.)

VEHICLE IMPOUNDED? ☐ YES ☐ NO   LOCATION:

NARRATIVE

NARRATIVE: (INCLUDE ACTIONS AND CONVERSATION BY SUSPECT(S) AND VICTIM(S) AND OTHER EVENTS NOT PREVIOUSLY COVERED)

WITNESS CHECK 1 ☐ YES 2 ☐ NO

CONTINUED ☐

52

Police Department

GENERAL CRIME REPORT

Grid

CASE NO.

VICTIM'S NAME (Last-First-Middle-Firm Name If Business)

1

X R

2

LOCATION

Classification

Property Owned or Controlled by	
Premises Secured by - Date - Time	Date - Time - Day Occurred	Date - Time - Day Reported to P.D.

Type of Property Taken or Attacked (Furs - Jewelry, etc.)

Value of Loss - Damage
$

If Citizen Arrest—Arrested by

Trade Mark of Suspects (Actions - Conversations)

Type of Premises Attacked (Motel - Alley - Service Station, etc.)

Method Used to Enter or Attack

Apparent Motive

Where Were Occupants?

Physical Evidence by (Inv's. Name)

Vehicle Used by Suspects (Year - Make - Body Type - Color - License and I.D. Nos.)

Victim's or Complainant's Occupation

Residence Address - City - Phone

Business Address - City - Phone - Occupation

Second Victim's Occupation

Witnesses - Name - Sex - Race - Age

1

2

3

Suspects   Address

Booking Charge and No. - If Not Booked - Ht. - Wt. - Hair - Eyes - Complx. - Other I.D. Characteristics)

1

2

3

4

LOSS Item No.	(1) Itemize Loss (One Article to a line - List and Describe Fully - Serial Numbers and Values in Columns) (2) Identify Additional Suspects (3) Reconstruct the Crime (No Duplication of Prior Itemized Information) (4) Summarize Other Details Relating to the Crime	Serial Numbers	VALUE

VICTIM OR FAMILY NOTIFIED OF STATE INDEMNIFICATION POSSIBILITY ON _____ (DATE)

Copies to	Copies by	Indexed by	Approved	Officer ID No.	Date & Time

53

REFERRAL ☐   DATE ....

INFORMATION ☐   BC NO. ....

NAME OF CHILD ....

CURRENT WHEREABOUTS .... PHONE NO...........................

BIRTHDATE .... PLACE OF BIRTH ....

FATHER'S NAME .... ADDRESS.................................... PHONE NO...........................

MOTHER'S NAME.................................. ADDRESS.................................... PHONE NO...........................

STEPPARENT(S)...................................... ADDRESS.................................... PHONE NO...........................

SIBLINGS' NAMES (Use reverse side if necessary)   BIRTHDATES

1. ....

2. ....

3. ....

4. ....

5. ....

DATE OF INJURY .... INFLICTED BY ....

DATE OF INJURY OBSERVED OR KNOWN .... REPORTED BY ....

TYPE OF INJURY..

SEEN BY DR. Yes ☐   NAME AND ADDRESS ....
             No ☐

WITNESSES' NAMES & ADDRESSES ....

....

ACTION TAKEN ....

COMMENTS:

IN CASE OF EMERGENCY OR OBVIOUS BATTERING, THE LOCAL POLICE AUTHORITY SHOULD BE NOTIFIED IMMEDIATELY.

The battered child report, Probation Form No. 516, is a dual purpose form. It is to be used in reporting those instances of non-accidental injury required by Section 11161.5 of the Penal Code. These referrals require an investigation to determine if official action should be taken to protect the child.

The form is also for reporting those cases not covered by the Penal Code, those marginal "grey area" situations where there is suspicion or concern that the children may be subjected to abuse. No official action will be taken on these reports unless it becomes apparent that a child's safety is in jeopardy.

Probation Form No. 516 should be filled out as completely as possible. On referrals, the original is to be sent to the Probation Department, the first carbon to the police agency and the second copy retained by the reporting agency or person. If a report is being forwarded for information only, the original is to be sent to the Probation Department and the additional copies destroyed.

The sending party should check the appropriate box in the upper left hand corner and fill in the date. The BC number will be added at the Probation Department. The legal name of the child and any names by which he may be known should be listed. The current whereabouts and phone number should reflect the child's placement at the time of the referral, such as relative's home, University Hospital, etc.

The family information and information regarding the injury should be completed as fully as possible.

"Action taken" should indicate the immediate action at the time the injury was noticed.

In reporting information only, many of these items will not be applicable. The section for comments should be utilized to describe the problem or situation which led to the report being filed.

All reports should be forwarded without delay to **BC File, San Diego County Probation Department, Box 23096, San Diego, California 92123.**

MEDICAL REPORT – SUSPECTED CHILD ABUSE

INSTRUCTIONS: ALL PROFESSIONAL MEDICAL PERSONNEL ARE REQUIRED BY LAW TO COMPLETE THIS FORM WHERE CHILD ABUSE, AS DEFINED BY SECTION 11161.5 OF THE PENAL CODE, IS SUSPECTED AND SUBMIT IT TO EITHER THE LOCAL POLICE OR SHERIFF AND TO THE PROBATION DEPARTMENT, OR IN THE ALTERNATIVE TO EITHER THE WELFARE DEPARTMENT OR TO THE COUNTY HEALTH DEPARTMENT WITHIN 36 HOURS. PROFESSIONAL MEDICAL PERSONNEL MEANS ANY PHYSICIAN AND SURGEON, DENTIST, RESIDENT, INTERN, PODIATRIST, CHIROPRACTOR, PSYCHOLOGIST, RELIGIOUS PRACTITIONER FOR DIAGNOSIS, EXAMINATION OR TREATMENT; OR A REGISTERED NURSE IN THE EMPLOY OF A PUBLIC HEALTH AGENCY. EACH PART OF THE FORM MUST BE COMPLETED UNLESS INAPPLICABLE. IN FILLING OUT THIS FORM NO CIVIL LIABILITY ATTACHES AND NO CONFIDENTIALITY IS BREACHED.

I. GENERAL INFORMATION   Print or type

PATIENT'S NAME	HOSPITAL ID NO.

ADDRESS	CITY	COUNTY	STATE	PHONE

AGE	BIRTHDATE	RACE	SEX	DATE & TIME OF ARRIVAL	MODE OF TRANSPORTATION	DATE & TIME OF DISCHARGE

ACCOMPANIED TO HOSPITAL BY: NAME	ADDRESS	CITY	STATE	RELATIONSHIP

PHONE REPORT MADE TO	ID NO.	DEPARTMENT	PHONE	RESPONDING OFFICER/AGENCY

NAME OF: ☐ FATHER ☐ STEPFATHER	ADDRESS	CITY	COUNTY	HOME PHONE	BUS. PHONE	AGE/DOB

NAME OF: ☐ MOTHER ☐ STEPMOTHER	ADDRESS	CITY	COUNTY	HOME PHONE	BUS. PHONE	AGE/DOB

SIBLINGS: LAST NAME, FIRST	DOB	LAST NAME, FIRST	DOB	LAST NAME, FIRST	DOB

II. MEDICAL EXAMINATION

A. History   1. EXPLANATION OF INJURIES BY PARENT OR PERSON ACCOMPANYING CHILD (LOCATION, DATE, TIME & CIRCUMSTANCES)

2. PATIENT'S STATEMENT EXPLAINING INJURY (PARAPHRASE)

3. PATIENT'S EMOTIONAL REACTION TO EXAMINATION (SUBMISSIVE, COMPLIANT, ETC.)

4. PREVIOUS HISTORY OF CHILD ABUSE (IF KNOWN)

B. Sexual Assault   Perform exam only if necessary.

1. ACTS COMMITTED: NOTE — COITUS, FELLATIO, CUNNILINGUS, SODOMY

2. DURING ASSAULT
☐ VAGINAL PENETRATION (HOW)   EJACULATION: ☐ VAGINAL ☐ ORAL ☐ ANAL ☐ OTHER:
☐ ANAL PENETRATION (HOW)   ☐ CONDOM USED ☐ VOMITED ☐ LOSS OF CONSCIOUSNESS ☐ OTHER:

3. AFTER ASSAULT:
☐ WIPED/WASHED ☐ BATHED ☐ DOUCHED ☐ VOMITED ☐ CHANGED CLOTHES ☐ BRUSHED TEETH ☐ DEFECATED ☐ OTHER:

C. Physical Examination	DATE & TIME OF EXAM	DATE & TIME OF ASSAULT	BP	PULSE	RESP.	TEMP

HEIGHT	WEIGHT	HEAD CIRCUM	LAST TETANUS	KNOWN ALLERGIES	CURRENT MEDICATION

DIAGNOSTIC DATA

Check if indicated and incorporate results in written examination at left

☐ X–Rays (skull, chest, longbone, full skeletal)

☐ Bleeding, coagulation, tourniquet, tests

☐ Funduscopic

☐ Other

PHYSICAL EXAMINATION (CONTINUED) LOCATE AND DESCRIBE IN DETAIL ANY INJURIES OR FINDINGS; TRAUMA, BRUISES, ERYTHEMA, EXCORIATIONS, LACERATIONS, WOUNDS. TRACE OUT LINE USED & INDICATE LOCATION OF WOUNDS/LACERATIONS USING 'X' FOR SUPERFICIAL, 'O' FOR DEEP, SHADE FOR BRUISES OR BURNS. BESIDE EACH INJURY INDICATED NOTE COLOR, SIZE, PATTERN, TEXTURE, AND SENSATION. WRITE OVER UNUSED OUTLINES. DESCRIBE IN DETAIL SHAPE OF ARM OR OTHER BRUISES WHICH MAY INDICATE FORCE.

D. PELVIC A PELVIC EXAMINATION SHOULD NOT BE PERFORMED UNLESS THE PARENT, GUARDIAN OR MINOR CONSENT OR UNLESS NECESSARY AS PART OF TREATMENT. SEE DEPARTMENT OF HEALTH REGULATIONS TITLE 22, DIVISION 2, VICTIMS OF SEXUAL ASSAULT. SAME INSTRUCTIONS AS GENERAL PHYSICAL; IN ADDITION, NOTE PUBIC HAIR COMBINGS WHERE INDICATED, DRIED SECRETIONS & RECENT INJURIES TO HYMEN, TRACE & OUTLINE AS ABOVE.

V. SPECIMENS

STAINS/FOREIGN MATERIALS (WHEN INDICATED)

LOOSE HAIR ___	FINGERNAIL SCRAPINGS ___
BLOOD ___	DIRT OR GRAVEL ___
THREADS ___	VEGETATION ___
GRASS ___	CLOTHING ___
DRIED SECRETIONS ___	

	SLIDES	SWABS
VAGINAL	___	___
RECTAL	___	___
ORAL	___	___
ASPIRATES/ WASHINGS	___	___
BITE MARKS	___	___
OTHER:	___	___

PATIENT'S SAMPLES, TIME OF COLLECTION AT MD DISCRETION

BLOOD	___
HAIR FROM HEAD	___
SALIVA	___
HAIR FROM PUBIC AREA	___

III. DIAGNOSTIC IMPRESSION OF TRAUMA AND INJURIES

IV. TREATMENT/DISPOSITION OF PATIENT

A. ☐ GC CULTURE ☐ VDRL ☐ PREGNANCY TEST ☐ POST COITAL ESTROGEN ☐ VD PRO- PHYLAXIS ☐ OTHER:

☐ MOTILE SPERM: ☐ PRESENCE ☐ ABSENCE ☐ NOT TAKEN FAMILY ASSESSMENT BY: ☐ NOT ORDERED

B. ORDERS:

C. DISPOSITION: ☐ ADMIT   TRANSFERRED TO:

☐ RELEASED   ACCOMPANIED BY: NAME   ADDRESS   RELATIONSHIP

D. FOLLOW—UP WITHIN:

☐ MEDICAL

☐ SOCIAL SERVICES ___ HRS ___ DAYS

☐ PRIVATE MD ___ HRS ___ DAYS

☐ OTHER ___ HRS ___ DAYS

___ HRS ___ DAYS

I HAVE RECEIVED THE INDICATED ITEMS AS EVIDENCE AND A COPY OF THIS REPORT.

OFFICER: ID NO.:   DATE:

NURSE   SIGNATURE OF EXAMINING PHYSICIAN

MEDICAL REPORT-SUSPECTED SEXUAL ASSAULT

PRINT OR TYPE   FORM 923

HOSPITAL

I. GENERAL INFORMATION

A.	PATIENT'S NAME			HOSPITAL ID NO.	

	ADDRESS		CITY	COUNTY	STATE	PHONE
B.						

	AGE	BIRTHDATE	RACE (USE CODED SUB-GROUPS)	SEX	DATE AND TIME OF ARRIVAL	MODE OF TRANSPORTATION
C.						

	ACCOMPANIED BY: NAME	ADDRESS	CITY	COUNTY	STATE	PHONE	RELATIONSHIP
D.							

	OFFICER NO. 1	ID NO.	DEPARTMENT	PHONE
E.				
	OFFICER NO.	ID NO.	DEPARTMENT	PHONE

II. PATIENT'S or PARENT'S or GUARDIAN'S CONSENT (Sign where indicated)

I UNDERSTAND THAT HOSPITALS AND PHYSICIANS ARE REQUIRED BY PENAL CODE SECTION 11160-11161.5 TO REPORT TO LAW ENFORCEMENT AUTHORITIES THE NAME AND WHEREABOUTS OF ANY PERSONS WHO ARE VICTIMS OF SEXUAL ASSAULT OR WHO HAVE SUFFERED INJURIES INFLICTED BY A DEADLY WEAPON OR IN VIOLATION OF A PENAL LAW AND THE TYPE AND EXTENT OF THOSE INJURIES. KNOWING THIS, I CONSENT TO INDICATED TREATMENT.

_____
PATIENT OR PARENT OR GUARDIAN

I FURTHER UNDERSTAND THAT A SEPARATE MEDICAL EXAMINATION FOR EVIDENCE OF SEXUAL ASSAULT AT PUBLIC EXPENSE CAN, WITH MY CONSENT, BE CONDUCTED BY THE TREATING PHYSICIAN TO DISCOVER AND PRESERVE EVIDENCE OF THE ASSAULT. IF SO CONDUCTED, THE REPORT OF THE EXAMINATION AND ANY EVIDENCE OBTAINED WILL BE RELEASED TO LAW ENFORCEMENT. KNOWING THIS, I CONSENT TO A MEDICAL EXAMINATION FOR EVIDENCE OF SEXUAL ASSAULT.

_____
PATIENT OR PARENT OR GUARDIAN

III. FINANCIAL RESPONSIBILITY OF LOCAL GOVERNMENT (Government Code Section 13961.5)

I HEREBY REQUEST A MEDICAL EXAMINATION & COLLECTION OF EVIDENCE FOR SUSPECTED SEXUAL ASSAULT OF THE ABOVE PATIENT AT PUBLIC EXPENSE.

OFFICER	ID NO.	DATE

IV. MEDICAL EXAMINATION

A. HISTORY	ANSWER LINES 4-6 YES OR NO, OR EXPLAIN FOR EACH CATEGORY.	1. DATE AND TIME OF EXAM	DATE AND TIME OF ASSAULT

2. PHYSICAL SURROUNDINGS (BED, FIELD, CAR, ETC.)   IF PHYSICALLY RESTRAINED, HOW

3. PATIENT'S DESCRIPTION OF ASSAULT AND ASSOCIATED PAIN (PARAPHRASE)

NAME(S) AND NUMBER OF ASSAILANT(S)

WEAPON USED (GUN, KNIFE, ETC.)   IF FOREIGN OBJECT USED, WHAT AND WHERE

4. ACTS COMMITTED	COITUS	FELLATIO	CUNNILINGUS	SODOMY

5. DURING ASSAULT	VAGINAL PENETRATION (HOW)		EJACULATION: ☐ VAGINAL ☐ ORAL ☐ ANAL	☐ OTHER:
	☐ ANAL PENETRATION (HOW)	☐ CONDOM USED	☐ VOMITED ☐ LOSS OF CONSCIOUSNESS	☐ OTHER:

6. AFTER ASSAULT	☐ WIPED/WASHED ☐ BATHED ☐ DOUCHED ☐ VOMITED ☐ CHANGED CLOTHES ☐ BRUSHED TEETH ☐ DEFECATED
	☐ OTHER:

7. MENSTRUAL HISTORY:

8.	BP	PULSE	TEMP.	RESP.	KNOWN ALLERGIES

CURRENT MEDICATION   LAST TETANUS

B. GENERAL PHYSICAL	1. PATIENT'S GENERAL PHYSICAL APPEARANCE	HEIGHT	WEIGHT	

61926-582 6-76 100M OSP

58

B. GENERAL PHYSICAL (Cont.)

2. LOCATE & DESCRIBE IN DETAIL ANY INJURIES OR FINDINGS (SPECULUM & BIMANUAL EXAM): TRAUMA, BRUISES, ERYTHEMA, EXCORIATIONS, LACERATIONS, WOUNDS, STAINS/FOREIGN MATERIALS ON BODY-MUCOID OR LIQUID MATERIAL, LOOSE HAIR, BLOOD, GRASS, DIRT, ETC.

TRACE OUTLINE USED & INDICATE LOCATION OF WOUNDS/LACERATIONS, USING 'X' FOR SUPERFICIAL, 'O' FOR DEEP; SHADE FOR BRUISES. WRITE OVER UNUSED OUTLINES. DESCRIBE IN DETAIL SHAPE OF BRUISES (ON ARMS OR OTHER EXTREMITIES) WHICH MAY INDICATE FORCE.

C. PELVIC

IF A CHILD, PERFORM ONLY IF NECESSARY.(SAME INSTRUCTIONS AS GENERAL PHYSICAL; IN ADDITION, NOTE PUBIC HAIR COMBINGS, DRIED SECRETIONS AND RECENT INJURIES TO HYMEN WHERE INDICATED.) TRACE AND MARK OUTLINE AS ABOVE.

V. DIAGNOSTIC IMPRESSION OF TRAUMA AND INJURIES

VI. TREATMENT/DISPOSITION OF PATIENT

A. ☐ GC CULTURE ☐ VDRL ☐ PREGNANCY TEST ☐ POST COITAL ESTROGEN ☐ VD PRO-PHYLAXIS ☐ OTHER:

B. ORDERS:

MOTILE SPERM: ☐ PRESENCE ☐ ABSENCE ☐ NOT TAKEN

C. DISPOSITION: ☐ ADMIT   TRANSFERRED TO

D. FOLLOW-UP WITHIN: ☐ MEDICAL   ☐ SOCIAL SERVICES   ☐ PRIVATE MD   ☐ OTHER

HOURS DAYS   HOURS DAYS   HOURS DAYS   HOURS DAYS

ACCOMPANIED BY: NAME   ADDRESS   RELATIONSHIP

☐ RELEASED

I HAVE RECEIVED THE INDICATED ITEMS AS EVIDENCE AND A COPY OF THIS REPORT.

OFFICER: ID NO.:   DATE:

NURSE   SIGNATURE OF EXAMINING PHYSICIAN

VII. SPECIMENS

STAINS/FOREIGN MATERIALS (WHEN INDICATED)

LOOSE HAIR ___	FINGERNAIL SCRAPINGS ___
BLOOD ___	DIRT OR GRAVEL ___
THREADS ___	VEGETATION ___
GRASS ___	CLOTHING ___

DRIED SECRETIONS ___

	SLIDES	SWABS
VAGINAL	___	___
RECTAL	___	___
ORAL	___	___
ASPIRATES/WASHINGS	___	___
BITE MARKS	___	___
OTHER:	___	___

PATIENT'S SAMPLES, TIME OF COLLECTION AT MD DISCRETION.

BLOOD	___
HAIR FROM HEAD	___
SALIVA	___
HAIR FROM PUBIC AREA	___

61928-982 6-76 100M OSP

SEX ABUSE HISTORY AND PHYSICAL EXAMINATION CHECK OFF SHEET #1

A check mark is to be used to indicate that that part of the history and physical examination has received attention. If further description is needed, please write in the space provided.

STAMP

SEX ABUSE HISTORY

Name _____ Sex: ☐ M ☐ F DOB _____

Date: _____ Time: _____ Witness(es): _____

_____

CC: _____ Time: _____ Date: _____

Location: _____

Consent Yes ☐ No ☐ Explain:
for history & physical?

Circumstances:

☐ Witnesses?

☐ Previous intercourse? When? _____

☐ Menses

☐ Contraception? ☐ He ☐ She

☐ Recent: ☐ defecation When: _____

  ☐ washing _____

  ☐ douching _____

  ☐ voiding _____

  ☐ eating/drinking _____

PHYSICAL EXAMINATION

☐ General: Temperature _____ Pulse _____ Resp. _____ BP _____

☐ Affect:

☐ Clothes: ☐ tears ☐ stains ☐ remove

60

Children's Hospital and Health Center
| 8001 FROST STREET | SAN DIEGO | CALIFORNIA 92123 |

Sex Abuse History and Physical Examination Check Off Sheet - #2

Physical Examination, continued

☐ Skin: ☐ stains ☐ lacerations

☐ scratches ☐ rash

☐ bruises ☐ blood

☐ temperature ☐ moisture

☐ bites ☐ other lesions (insects, etc.)

STAMP

☐ Nails

☐ Hair

☐ Scalp

☐ Eyes

☐ Ears

☐ Nose

☐ Mouth: ☐ gums ☐ teeth

☐ mucosa ☐ discharge

☐ odor ☐ lesions

☐ Throat: ☐ lesions

☐ discharge

☐ infection

☐ Chest: ☐ heart

☐ lungs

☐ Abdomen

☐ Perineum: ☐ secretions and/or ☐ discharge

☐ swelling

☐ bruising

☐ lacerations

☐ hair (comb)

Sex Abuse History and Physical Examination Check Off Sheet - #3

Physical Examination, continued

STAMP

☐ Perineum, continued: ☐ labia maj.

☐ labia min.

☐ hymen

☐ vagina   Size: _____   ☐ tears:

☐ Pelvic Examination: ☐ vaginal wall

☐ fundus

☐ adnexae

☐ introitus

☐ Pelvic Examination: ☐ tears

☐ digital

☐ Thighs

☐ Extremities: ☐ deformities

☐ bruises

☐ lacerations

☐ stains

Note: It is recognized that this history does not satisfy the requirements of the Police as to assailant's description, modus operandi, identifying characteristics, etc., but it is not intended as such. This history sheet is intended to be used as the physician's guide for the pertinent examination and collection of crucial evidence.

STAMP

SEXUAL ABUSE LABORATORY CHECK OFF AND ORDER SHEET #1

Specimens delivered by: _____ R.N.

Specimens received by: _____ M.T., Supervisor

Time Received: _____ AM _____ PM

Billing **BLOOD**
Code

001 ☐ CBC _____ HgB _____ Hct _____ WBC

Diff: | PMN | Bands | Lymphs | Monos | Eos | Basos | Others

286 ☐ VDRL - repeat two weeks

176 ☐ Blood Type

967 or 976 ☐ Toxicology Screen - ETOH, Barbiturates, Valium, Other

_____ ☐ Other - i.e., test for sickle cell disease

URINE

145 ☐ U.A. with micro   Occult   Differential   Other
         pH   S.G.   Blood   WBC   RBC   Sperm

303 ☐ Pregnancy test - repeat 8 weeks

486 & 487 ☐ Acid Phosphatase

967 or 976 ☐ Toxicology Screen

_____ ☐ Other - i.e., sperm, culture

☐ Saliva - secretors - to be done in Police Laboratory

SWAB FOR G.C. CULTURE AND GRAM STAIN

351 & 340 ☐ Mouth

351 & 340 ☐ Vagina

351 & 340 ☐ Rectum

351 & 340 ☐ Pharynx

_____ ☐ Other - i.e., Bartholin's glands

WHITE: Examining Physician / Yellow: Laboratory / Pink & Gold: CPT Chart

CHILDREN'S HOSPITAL AND HEALTH CENTER
| 8001 FROST STREET | SAN DIEGO | CALIFORNIA 92123 |

SEXUAL ABUSE LABORATORY CHECK OFF AND ORDER SHEET - #2

Billing
Code   SPERM CYTOLOGY

232   ☐   Wet Mount   ☐   Spray-fixed, wet mount

           ☐   Vaginal Washing   ☐   Mouth   ☐   Other, i.e., dress

           ☐   Mouth   ☐   Anus   thigh, etc.

           ☐   Urine   ☐   Vagina   ☐   Rectum

_____   ☐   Pap Smear

         ☐   <u>VAGINAL ASPIRATION OR WASHINGS</u>

             ☐   Semen

                 ☐   ABO Ags - To Police Laboratory

_____   ☐   Sperm - motility usually no ⟩2 hours; possible up to 24 hours

                   ⌐ cytology - usually no ⟩6 hours; possible up to 48 hours

487   ☐   Acid Phosphatase (50 K.A. units is diagnostic)

                ☐   Precipitation test vs. human sperm - to Police Laboratory

351   ☐   G.C. Culture

_____   ☐   Other Culture

         ☐   <u>U.V. Light - Semen, wet or dry</u>

         ☐   <u>Debris from clothing - to Police Laboratory</u>

         ☐   <u>Comb - pubic hair(s) - to Police Laboratory</u>

343   ☐   <u>Stool - hematest</u>

NOTE: Not all laboratory tests will be done in every case. Selection must be made according to history and physical circumstances.

Time of specimen collection: _____ AM   _____ PM

Specimens collected by: _____ M.D.

Specimens given to and received by: _____ R.N.

Specimens reviewed by: _____ M.D.,
                                                 Pathologist

WHITE: Examining Physician / YELLOW: Laboratory / PINK & GOLD: CPT Chart

Chapter 10

Child Abuse and the M.D.

by David L. Chadwick, M.D.
Children's Hospital San Diego, California

Although friends often are curious about child abuse, it is unusual for patients to ask about it. The abusive parent in the physician's office may ask for help in indirect ways but rarely asks for information about abuse. Child abuse, as a disease, is in the same stage that venereal disease was a generation ago. The person who thinks he may have it is not eager to discuss it with anyone and is likely to approach the problem obliquely. Abused infants and children are often brought to the physician for care, but the person who brings them often comes with a complaint that has nothing to do with the obvious injury. With notable exceptions, the medical profession has not distinguished itself in recognizing child abuse. This is understandable, since little or no attention was given to the subject in medical school until recent years. Today, many educational programs are offered concerning child abuse, but it is only one subject among many that clamor for the attention of busy practitioners.

Family practitioners and pediatricians need to know about child abuse. Neurosurgeons, orthopedists, and general and pediatric surgeons should know the syndromes of child abuse as they occur in their specialities. Psychiatrists should understand the dynamics of child abuse. Primary-care physicians who intend to deal with abused children need to learn five vital aspects of their care; recognition, reporting, helping the child, helping the family, and helping the community.

Recognition

When an abused child is brought to a physician, the family rarely gives a history of purposeful injury. They complain of an illness or mention an accident. Recognition of nonaccidental injury may be based on one of the pathognomonic injuries such as "corner" fractures, posterior rib fractures, spiral fractures of long bones, cigarette burns or scars, buttock striped scars, or injuries that are discrepant with the history given. Injuries accompanied by signs of neglect should also arouse suspicion. Almost any injury in an infant less than 1 year of age should make the physician think of child abuse.

In cases of possible child abuse, where doubt exists, consultation is indicated. Like any other diagnosis, it may be difficult to recognize the first time one sees it. Most cities now have child abuse consultants who are willing to review cases with physicians by telephone without charge and assist in ruling abuse in or out. A few cases always remain "gray," but 95% of the time it is possible to make this diagnosis or exclude it. An experienced pediatric radiologist often can diagnose nonaccidental injury from the skeletal survey without ever seeing the infant or talking to the family.

Missing the diagnosis of child abuse can be fatal for the child. Without any clear statistical proof, I am convinced that many more infants die of "missed abuse" than of "missed meningitis." Perhaps more important than the deaths are the permanently damaged children who will require special care all of their lives.

Reporting

Reporting suspected nonaccidental injuries is required by law in every state. The reporting statutes vary somewhat, but any district attorney's office can inform a physician about the details of the local law. Most reporting laws have provisions that protect the sincere reporter from civil liability and most make failure to report a misdemeanor. The most serious hazard stems from civil liability for failure to report. Thus, a California court awarded $400,000 to a child who was permanently brain-damaged by abuse subsequent to a nonaccidental injury for which he had been seen by a physician. The $400,000 came from the physician's insurance carrier.

Helping the Child

Medical care for the injuries the child has received is an obvious need, and most physicians need no advice in giving or arranging for such care. Next, the physician must concern himself with protecting the child from subsequent injury. This is often difficult, involving interaction with judges, social workers, and even attorneys. If the physician finds this too distasteful, he should find another physician who is willing to do it. The physician who fails to deal with the legal and social persons who exist for this purpose is absolutely useless to his patient.

Another responsibility is to see that the child has careful medical, developmental, and psychological care. Children who have been abused are a high risk for a variety of problems and usually need much help—the physician should see that they get it.

Helping the Family

Far too many physicians still take a hostile, punitive attitude toward parents who have abused their children. No one would argue that society in general, or physicians in particular, should condone child abuse, but if the physician's task is to heal, how can he ignore the extraordinary needs of these families for healing? Further, our cities abound with district attorneys, police, and judges—all fully capable of investigating, charging, judging, and sentencing these people. There is no need for the physician to perform their functions.

From the time the doctor recognizes nonaccidental injuries he should adopt a supportive attitude toward the family. He should inform them that the law requires him to report the injuries. He should then offer his sympathetic services to the mother, father, or other guardian in seeking help for their problems, usually through a social worker attached to a welfare agency, but sometimes through a psychiatrist or other skilled, informed professional. The physician should identify the other professionals in his community who are experienced and effective, and he should make informed referrals just as he would for other medical problems.

The "ideal" outcome of a case of serious child abuse is that the infant recovers from the injuries and is able to be safely replaced in his home without fear of subsequent injury. Today, such outcomes are rare, and the most common "solution" is prolonged out-of-home placement. While this outcome is better than death or permanent disability, it still leaves a lot to be desired.

Helping the Community

Successful management of a single case of child abuse usually requires involvement of many agencies and disciplines. Dealing with the problem as a whole may involve as many as 20 or 30 agencies in a

67

large city. This offers physicians a golden opportunity to become involved in the affairs of their community in a positive way. A physician's involvement in child abuse programs is usually gratefully accepted and his contributions can be the key to community actions leading to more effective prevention and treatment.

The doctor will not always see eye-to-eye with the policeman, the social worker, or the district attorney, nor is he expected to do so. As long as all parties respect one another's special expertise and individual value, multidisciplinary committees may work.

The physician can analyze child abuse as he would analyze a complex disease. He can imbue other professionals with his own analytical attitude and assist his community to use its resources in the most effective manner. It is important that this be done, since in our present state of knowledge, the rehabilitation of abusive parents is time-consuming and expensive. Few communities can afford to waste resources on ineffective "therapeutic" measures such as criminal prosecution. Still, many communities do waste their efforts in this way while failing to provide adequate child protective services, hot-lines for stressed parents, intensive support of possible abusers, and other preventative measures.

Prevention of child abuse is a real possibility, and I suspect that many cases are already being prevented by intelligent measures. Well-established predisposing factors include a history that the parent was himself abused, social isolation, unrealistic expectations of the infant, inability to seek or use help, and a personality best described as deeply unlikeable. Parents demonstrating two or three of these features and who have or who are expecting babies or adopting young children should be offered help before acts of abuse have occurred. The conventional psychiatric approach that says "Come to me and I will help you" will not work with such parents. Help must be pushed on them, and the helper needs to be both skilled and capable of tolerating repeated rejection before a therapeutic relationship is established. Every community needs to develop a staff of persons who have the necessary skills. Often, they are best located in a county welfare department of protective services, but this is a matter of individual community choice. They rarely can function in the private sector, since many families cannot or will not pay for this kind of service. It is my belief that the costs of caring for child abuse including the acute medical care of the children, the custodial care of the permanently damaged child, the remedial care of the temporarily handicapped child, the prosecution of parents, the civil proceedings required for protection of children, and the psychiatric care of families are high and mounting rapidly. More support needs to go into identification and care of the high-risk parent who has not yet abused an infant.

To sum it up, doctors can do much about child abuse. Their services are essential to recognition of cases and most important in reporting, helping the child, helping the family, and helping the community. If his efforts are to be effective, the physician must take the trouble to become informed about the problem.

Chapter 11

Common Medical Terms Associated with Child Abuse Cases

ABRASION—a scraping wound.

BONE—regions or areas of long bones each derived from a separate growth center.
   a. epiphysis—the end
   b. metaphysis—between the end (above) and the shaft.
   c. diaphysis—the shaft

BURN—stages of severity:
   a. first degree—scorching or painful redness of the skin.
   b. second degree—blister formation.
   c. third degree—destruction of outer layers of skin; may need skin grafting to permit healing.

CONCUSSION—an injury of a soft structure resulting from violent shaking or jarring.
   a. brain concussion—an injury characterized by immediate and transient impairment of brain function, e.g., alteration of consciousness or disturbance in vision and equilibrium.

CONGENITAL—existing at, and usually before birth; referring to conditions that are present at birth regardless of their causation.

CONTUSION—a wound producing damage of soft tissues with bleeding into surrounding tissues and tissue death.
   a. brain contusion—a structural damage to the brain, usually involving the outer surface. Cerebral edema (brain swelling) may or may not be present.
   b. scalp contusion—a wound with bleeding into or below the skin without gross disruption of the skin.

ENCOPRESIS—involuntary passes of feces; "soiling"

ENURESIS—involuntary passage of urine.

FAILURE TO THRIVE—a medical diagnosis based on comparison of the child's physical measurements and growth rates with those of the general population of children. When a child falls within the lowest three percent in weight, height and growth rates, the child is "failing to thrive."

FRACTURE—(to break)
- a. simple fracture—uncomplicated.
- b. compound fracture—an open wound of soft tissues which connects directly to fracture site.
- c. comminuted fracture—bone is broken into a number of pieces.
- d. spiral fracture—one in which the line of break runs obliquely up one side of the bone (as in a spiral staircase).
- e. torus fracture—a folding, bulging or buckling fracture.

HEMATEMESIS—vomiting of blood from stomach.

HEMATURIA—blood in the urine.

HEMOPTYSIS—spitting or coughing up of blood from windpipe or lungs.

INTRADEMAL HEMORRHAGE—(bleeding within the skin; doesn't blanch with pressure.)
- a. petechia—a round discrete hemorrhagic area less than 2mm (or 3/32″).
- b. ecchymosis—a hemorrhagic area larger than petechia.
- c. purpura—either petechia or ecchymosis, occurring in groups. They do not elevate the skin or mucosa.
- d. hematoma—underlying hemorrhage produces elevation of the skin or mucosa and discoloration is frequently seen. (bruise)

LAB TESTS
- a. Partial thromboplastin time (P.T.T.): measure of clotting factors.
- b. Prothrombin time (P.T.): circulating in the blood.
- c. platelet count—measure of the cellular component of blood involved in clotting.
- d. Urine analysis—examination of urine.
- e. Complete blood count (CBC)—measure of white and red cellular components in blood.
- f. Rumpel-Leede (Tourniquet) Test—a measure of capillary fragility and/or bruisability.

LACERATION—a cutting wound.

PERIOSTEAL ELEVATION—the outer growing layer of bone (periosteum) is displaced from the underlying bone by one of several processes which usually involve hemorrhage into the newly created space.

REFERENCE TERMS
    a. anterior—toward front
    b. distal—far (relative to proximal)
    c. frontal—front to head
    d. lateral—toward side
    e. medial—toward middle or mid-line
    f. occipital—back of head
    g. posterior—toward back
    h. proximal—near (near trunk)
    i. temporal—side of head

RETINAL HEMORRHAGE—bleeding from the inner lining of the eye.

SUBDURAL—usually refers to subdural hematoma, a hemorrhagic collection under one of the outer coverings of the brain (dura). Epidural hematoma (epi = above)—blood above the dura.

SUDDEN INFANT DEATH SYNDROME—the death of an apparently healthy infant which remains unexplained after a complete postmortem. Not child abuse related, only mistaken to be.

SUTURES—the meeting or joining of areas of bones in the skull. Separation of the sutures occurs with increased pressure within the skull as in a subdural hematoma.

Chapter 12

Injuries Frequently Found in Child Abuse Cases

by James Apthorpe, M.D.
Children's Hospital Los Angeles, California

I. Bruises
  A. Normal
    1. Knees-shins-single body, surface plane.
    2. One on forehead or chin.
  B. Non-accidental interior or front side of body.
    1. Multiple plane of body simultaneously.
    2. Both sides of face, etc.
      –injury on more than one plane is not consistent with one fall.
      –injury on one plane will be consistent with fall.
    3. Bruises on posterior or backside is unusual, particularly on back of thighs.
      a. Posterior most likely to be inflicted.
      b. Multiplicity of injuries.
  C. Hematoma
    1. Trapped blood.
  D. Ecchymosis—bruises
    1. Shape of bruises or imprint.
      a. Belt buckle, linear marks.
      b. Hand imprint—dots from finger tips, five round marks might be a squeeze.
II. Age
  A. Pediatrics—Science of child development.
    1. Development size and weight per age.

B. Limited explanations for injuries to infants.
   1. Child rarely bruises or breaks bones in a crib.
   2. Child 3 or 4 months of age left on a bassinette or bed—
      can roll off. (Child that falls on carpet usually won't be
      bruised or cut.)
      a. Injuries sustained in a free fall to floor or flat sur-
         face do not break legs may hit head and cause in-
         jury.
   3. Trauma to head can be accidental.
C. Story or history. Must be consistent with visible injury.
   1. When, how, etc., time and date.
D. Illness can cause bruises and some posterior.
   —example hemophillia
   1. Evaluate bruises by laboratory blood tests.
   2. Five screening tests which rule out bleeding diseases.
E. Cannot state amount of force to break bones or bruise.
   1. Takes more than normal contact, however.
F. Colorations of bruises.
   First red—in few minutes swollen in few hours turn blue-
   black dark look takes about 5 to 10 hours. In day or two
   turns lighter then, in approximately three days turns green-
   ish and then yellow. Within 5 days, light grayish-yellow.
III. Children can be injured without surface signs—kicked in stomach etc., because of soft tissue behind skin.
   Children can have serious injury to head without external trauma
   or visible injury.
   A. Shaking head can cause injuries. Brain substance soft-fluid
      pockets and spaces or surfaces—if blood accumulates be-
      tween it may damage brain.
      1. Brain contusion—when shaken or when struck may
         make brain shift and bruises and swells.
      2. Brain concussion—minor brain bruise, does not cause
         bleeding or permanent damage.
   B. Sub-dural hemotoma
      Acceleration or deceleration of brain may cause bounce back
      and injury on other side.
   C. Shaking child may cause severe injury to lower brain.

IV. Abdomen
   A. Many organs—some are solid.
      Example: Kidney, spleen, etc., are fixed and can be torn by blunt force without visible injury.
   B. Rupture of upper intestine can be ruptured by blunt force.
   C. These things can be identified as traumatic lesions—can be caused accidentally in older children.
V. Burns
   A. Difficult to evaluate.
      1. Cigarette burns—make same scar as chicken pox or infections, etc.
      2. Accidental burns. Must look at variables as to clothing and how burn occurred.
      3. Liquids
         a. Forced immersed.
            1. Depth of burn.
            2. Temperature of water and length of time emersed.
         b. Distribution of burns important.
            1. Symmetrical marks.
      4. Flame burns.
         a. Clothing important as to determine.
         b. Imprint to contact burns forced against heater, etc.
NOTE: Investigator should check height of heater and child—as well as patterns of burns, etc.
VI. Fracture
   A. Skull fracture alone without explanation is highly suspicious. Cannot be dated.
   B. Tubular or flat bones can be dated grossly.
   C. If bone has very sharp edges, it is fresh fracture—within three days they become rounded off.
   D. Calcium forms around break like splint.
   E. Fracture not visible in several years as completely renews.
   F. Skeletal Survey
      1. Usually swelling if at all in fracture will appear in hour or two.
      2. Two kinds of disease.
         a. Brittle bones—a very rare disease. Always have multiple fractures at birth and can be seen by x-ray.
         b. Second disease same as above but develops after birth.

G. Chip fracture—metaphaseal bone ends—being pulled off—cannot be accidental in infant—caused by pulled or by twisting.

H. Dislocation of bone in elbow by yanking child.

I. Spiral fracture
1. Slanting view of bone.
2. Twisting force needed.

J. Green stick or toras fracture.
1. Partial fracture.

NOTE: Infant should not have bruises or fractures. If so, should have a good story.

Chapter 13

The Dual Responsibility of Dentistry in Child Abuse

by Norman Sperber, DDS*

It has been estimated that as many as 2,000 American children will die this year, as a result of child abuse and neglect. And that's just the tip of the iceberg.

According to the California Department of Justice, Office of the Attorney General, "In California alone, more than 72,000 suspected cases of child maltreatment were reported in 1977 by the various agencies involved in the problem. However, the magnitude of child abuse and neglect is generally accepted as being much greater, since so many cases go unreported."[1]

As attention has focused on the tragic reality of child abuse in our society, experts have urged legislation that would mandate a wide range of skilled professionals to work together to help solve the problem.

At present, laws in each state require health and other professionals who work with children to report suspected incidents of child abuse to appropriate enforcement agencies. Such laws, coupled with the recent acceptance of bite marks as evidence by courts throughout the nation, have placed two new responsibilities upon dentistry.

Dentists are now responsible for clinically recognizing and reporting child abuse. The second responsibility is accepted by forensic odontologists who examine bite marks found on living and dead victims of child abuse.

Why Report Child Abuse?

According to the California Department of Justice, Office of the Attorney General, "Concern for the problem of the abused and ne-

---

*General practitioner, San Diego, and forensic odontologist for San Diego County Coroner's Office, Police Department, Sheriff's Department and District Attorney's Office.

glected child has reached national attention. No concern is more important to a community than the protection and welfare of its children. Babies and young children are among the most vulnerable victims of crime in California. Child abuse and neglect is an ugly reality, both a crime and a disease.

"Child abuse and neglect is found in all cultural, ethnic, occupational and socioeconomic groups. It is a problem that requires our immediate and serious attention and the development of interagency and community cooperative efforts in prevention education, reporting, training and treatment.

"Although the right of parents to control and raise their own children is accepted as a fundamental right in our society, intervention is justified by a paramount social interest—protection of the safety of the child. The Fourteenth Amendment of the United States Constitution states that everyone has equal protection under the law. Intervention for the protection of a child may involve a broad range of possible action including counseling and treatment, the filing of criminal charges, and/or the removal of a child from the control and custody of a parent, guardian or other caregiver.

"The serious and pervasive problem of child abuse and neglect is recognized and currently dealt with by a variety of disciplines. Many law enforcement and justice system personnel, the medical community, social service workers and others have developed strategies for handling the problem. Laws have been passed and enforced, medical diagnostic techniques discovered, counseling offered and direct services provided to families in difficulty.

"None of these strategies alone, however, can effectively combat child abuse. The communities that have established cooperation and communication among all the involved parties have learned that consistent, thorough and effective reporting, treatment and prevention of child abuse occurs when the expertise of all involved disciplines is utilized.

"The willful breaking of a child's leg by a parent or guardian is a physical assault by one human being upon another. It is clearly a crime and, as a result, those agencies of government responsible for dealing with crime must maintain a major role.

"Once such intervention has occurred, however, it is recognized that it may not always be appropriate to handle this type of criminal activity with a traditional crime and punishment approach. In making that decision, all segments of the system must work together to pool their collective experience and judgment in order to make the best decision. Only then can we be sure that the best interests of society, and particularly of the child, have been protected and served.

"Rather than any effort to compartmentalize our approaches to child abuse and neglect, we should all be moving to ensure even greater cooperation between law enforcement and social agencies as a team."[1]

What is Child Abuse?

Child abuse or nonaccidental injury is defined as "any act of omission or commission that endangers or impairs a child's physical or emotional health and development."

Child abuse is classified as follows:

- Physical abuse and corporal punishment:
  This type of abuse includes striking, shaking or throwing a child. Biting, burning, whipping, poking, cutting and twisting limbs are frequently encountered;
- Emotional abuse and deprivation:
  Includes emotional cruelty, lack of love;
- Physical neglect:
  Includes failure to provide food, shelter, clothing and professional care; failure of victim to thrive; and/or
- Sexual abuse and exploitation: Includes incestuous or intrafamilial relationships.

Dentists may encounter all of the above types of child abuse among their young patients, and are most likely to recognize physical abuse, deprivation and physical neglect.

The following approximations may be of value to the clinician:

Age and Sex Distribution of Victims in Child Abuse:

0–4 years of age—heaviest
5–8 years of age—less heavy
9–16 years of age—diminishes
Boys were abused more than girls by a 6:4 ratio

Age and Percentages of Abusing Parents:

Mothers 20 years and less—42%
Fathers 22 years and less—33%
One half of abusing parents have been married less than 2 years.
Males abused more than females by a 6:4 ratio.

Psychological Nature of Abusing Parents:

They may be immature and insecure. They may not relate well to other adults and may have frequent family crises. They may have been abused as children themselves. They may have drug, alcohol or related problems.

Clinical Recognition of Child Abuse

Any evidence of repeated trauma to the mouth, lips, jaws and teeth may be indicative of physical abuse. Healed or recent fractures of the maxilla and mandible should be carefully investigated.

A key factor that should lead to suspicion of child abuse is incompatibility of injuries with the account given by parents, guardians or the victims themselves.

As reported in the *Journal of the American Dental Association,* "Bruises, lacerations, burns, cuts, scars, large areas of ecchymosis and black eyes suggest physical abuse."

"These lesions are often produced on the face, neck and head of a child, in addition to other areas of the body. Arms and legs are often traumatized with severe contusions as well as occasional fractures of long bones. Trauma to the head, in addition to skull fractures, may produce extensive hematoma with swelling of the scalp. Severe ocular injuries are not uncommon and may include subconjunctival hemorrhages and detached retina.

"The mouth is often traumatized in cases of violent child abuse, particularly because of its psychological significance. Because children will cry or speak through the mouth, violence is used against the mouth to silence the child (Figure A).

"Scars on the lips should always alert the dentist to previous episodes of trauma, since lips rarely demonstrate scarring. Fractures of the maxilla or mandible should always be carefully investigated, since violent abuse must be ruled out in these cases. Missing teeth without obvious explanation should be investigated with intraoral radiographs in order to rule out some abnormality in sequence of tooth development and eruption.

"Child abuse with blows to the child's face usually results in tooth evulsion rather than tooth fracture, but fractures of crowns are easily observed, and fractures of tooth roots can be observed on intraoral radiographs. Multiple healed fractures of the tooth roots should always suggest trauma by abuse. Displaced teeth and unusual malocclusion also may suggest abnormal healing from previous traumatic experiences.

"And discolored teeth are suggestive of previous trauma with damage to the dental pulp. Abnormality of appearance and mobility of tongue may suggest scarring from severe traumatic experience—the tongue can be severely injured by the teeth in a blow to the mouth or jaw."[2]

Child abuse is not commonly observed in dental offices because children are not routinely seen before the ages of 2 or 3. Another reason dentists do not routinely see a great deal of physical abuse is that the face may be avoided by abusers because of its accessibility to public scrutiny. Most nonaccidental injuries to children are seen by physicians in private offices, clinics and hospitals.

Nonetheless, dentists are becoming more suspicious about the oral injuries they treat. They are being taught to question an injury to the teeth or oral structures that is not consistent with the history obtained from the parent or guardian.

The fact that failure to report child abuse is a misdemeanor in many states, punishable by imprisonment, fine or both, doubtlessly has attracted the attention of most health professionals. However, it is only fair to point out that, traditionally, dentists have been trained in prevention of dental disease, and it would be expected that as professionals, they would respond to prevention of death or serious injury through the early detection of nonaccidental injury. Thus it is anticipated that dentists in great numbers, through education and awareness, will join with other health professionals, educators, law enforcement agencies and other public guardians of the health and rights of the nation's children.

Reporting Child Abuse

While everyone should report suspected child abuse and neglect, it is a crime for certain professionals and lay personnel who have a special working relationship or contact with children not to report suspected abuse to the proper authorities.

Failure to report by telephone and in writing within 36 hours the observation of a . . . minor who has physical injury or injuries which appear to have been inflicted upon him by other than accidental means by any person, that the minor has been sexually molested or that any injury prohibited by terms of Section 273a has been inflicted upon the minor . . . to both the local police authority having jurisdiction and to the juvenile probation department; or, in the alternative either to the county welfare department or to the county health department . . . is a misdemeanor punishable by six months in jail or a $500 fine, or both.—*California Penal Code 11161.5.*

For those mandated to report who do not do so, there may also be civil liabilities.

Basically, this means that the law requires mandated reporters to report all suspected incidents of child abuse immediately to: 1) The local police *and* juvenile probation departments; or 2) The county welfare department or county health department.

"Those professionals required by this law to report are:

physicians
surgeons
dentists
residents
registered nurses
social workers
interns
podiatrists
chiropractors
religious practitioners
school superintendents
school principals
teachers
licensed day care workers
supervisors of child welfare and attendance
certificated pupil personnel employees (schools)
administrators of summer camps or child care centers

"These persons are not liable for either civil damages or criminal prosecution as a result of making a report, unless it is proven that they made a false report with malice."[1]

Bite Mark Evidence—
The Role of the Forensic Odontologist

The second charge for American dentists, and perhaps the more dramatic role, is the responsibility of a handful of the profession known as forensic odontologists. These dentists are specially trained and educated in a new discipline. They are a new breed, who, through objective principles and scientific procedures, are called upon to identify deceased individuals who *cannot* be recognized through the usual methods of visual, or fingerprint identification.

They are called upon to identify victims who have become mutilated, burned or decomposed. They understand the rules of evidence and are prepared to testify in the high courts of the land as expert witnesses in homicide, child abuse or sex crime cases. Forensic odontologists have been important members of identification teams in recent airline disasters.

A small number of forensic odontologists have had the opportunity to examine human bite marks found on victims and assailants (adults and children) dead and alive. Several convictions involving homicide, sexual crimes and child abuse have drawn on the objective findings of forensic odontologists as trial experts. Many of the cases included strong circumstantial evidence, but the inclusion of testimony of forensic odontologists aided the juries and the court in rendering verdicts based on physical data.

It is not uncommon to find bite marks on various parts of the bodies of abused children, whether dead or alive. The role of the forensic odontologist becomes quite important in such cases because often it is his or her testimony that identifies the abuser. Veteran investigators of child abuse know that family members, friends, or even the abused child will often shield the identity of abuser(s).

Bite marks may be either two- or three-dimensional. A two-dimensional bite mark can be recognized as one in which marks or stainings are observed below the skin surface (Figures B and C). Such a bite mark is usually compared with a suspect's teeth by matching life-sized photographs of the bite mark with overlays or transparencies traced from models or replicas of the suspect's teeth. (Figures D, E, F and G). (The reader may be able to reach some conclusions as to which suspect was more likely involved in the biting episode. This California case, homicide, resulted in the conviction of one of the suspects.)

The author of this article was prepared to testify in a child abuse case in which the father of the child was identified, through bite marks, as the abuser. While awaiting trial, the father denied involvement until the child, later, sustained a nonaccidental fracture of one arm while in the father's custody. At this point, the father admitted biting and abusing the child, whereupon the child was placed in a foster home. The case photographs (Figures H, I and J) in sequence, show the outlines on acetate of the suspect's teeth (blue), above, on and below the scarred bite marks (white). Note the apparent missing tooth on the bite mark. The absence of the tooth mark was due to a severe fracture of the left maxillary central incisor (#9). (A scale or ruler is used in all bite mark cases so that a life-sized photograph of the injury can be compared with life-sized models of the suspect's dentition.)

Videotape analysis and computer enhancement of bite mark evidence has been used in recent years in a number of cases throughout the United States.

In addition, experimental bite marks in wax, clay and other impression materials using models of the suspect are sometimes employed in an effort to compare them with the actual bite mark.

In the case of a third-dimensional bite mark (Figures K and L), there is an actual penetration of the skin. In such cases, comparisons can sometimes be made by an actual insertion of the model of the suspect's teeth into the bite mark depressions and comparison of overlays and photographs may be made as described earlier.

In any type of bite mark evidence, the forensic odontologist must constantly remember that the skin is not a perfect impression material. In many cases, he/she is looking at staining (hemorrhage) below the skin *caused* by the teeth, and *not* an actual mark caused by the teeth such as one may see in tool marks or fingerprint analysis. He/she must be aware of the factors of distortion and possible manipulation of the tissues during the commission of a bite.

Because they are uniquely able to determine evidence of child abuse, forensic odontologists, general practitioners and other dental specialists have the opportunity to become valued team members who

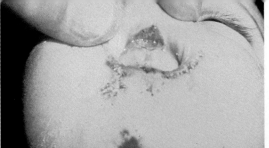

Dental Photos
A through G

Figure A. Typical oral manifestations of child abuse (homicide). (Photos by Norman Sperber, DDS.)

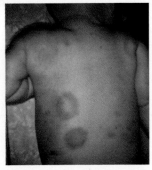

Figure B. Photo shows bite marks on victim (homicide).

Figure C. Arrow shows bite marks. Other signs of abuse are also evident on young victim's body.

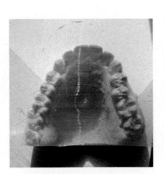

Figure D. An acetate overlay and outline of teeth over a model of a suspect's teeth.

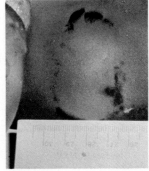

Figure E. Bite mark on shoulder of young homicide victim.

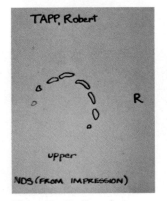

Figure F. Outline of one suspect's maxillary teeth.

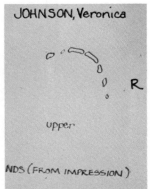

Figure G. Outline of maxillary teeth of another suspect in the same case.

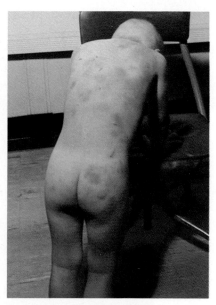

Fist blow to the forehead.

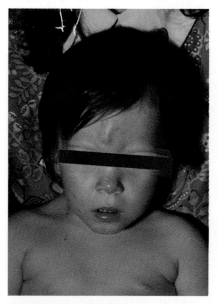

Strapping and trauma with fist.

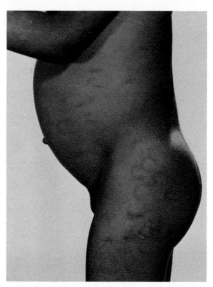

Multiple loop welts.

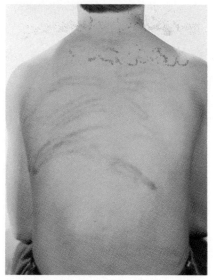

Velocity of extension cord causes long
narrow loop marks. Slower velocity
would widen the marks.

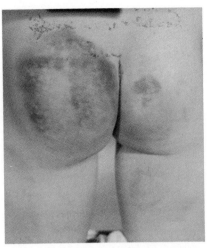

Spanking can be more than discipline.

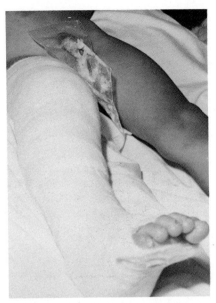

Little bones break easily. Broken leg could not be shown to be child abuse.

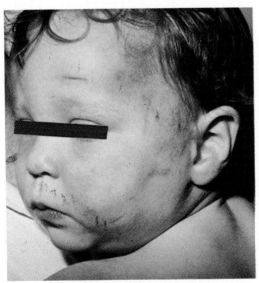

Multiple slaps to entire face and forehead.

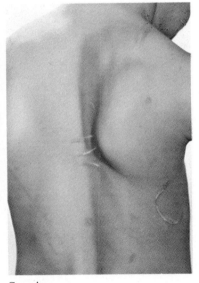

Scarring.

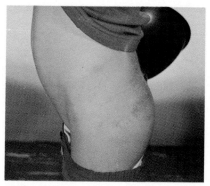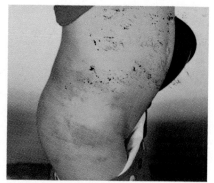

"Fell off bike"—Not a consistent injury. Both sides are hurt.

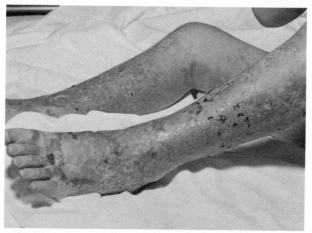

Child's legs submerged in tub of boiling water.

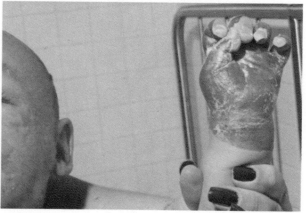

Dip burn.

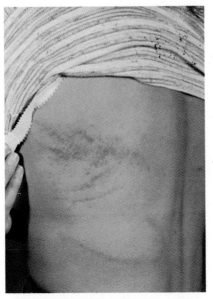

Cord whipping with blunt trauma blow.

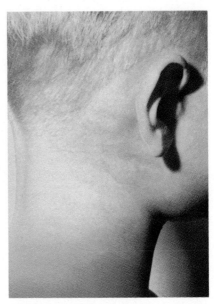

Bruises and blunt trauma.

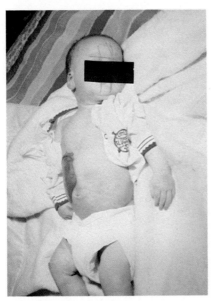

This child looked beaten but died of natural causes.

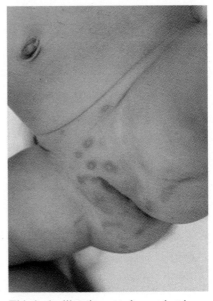

This looks like cigarette burns, but is a severe diaper rash.

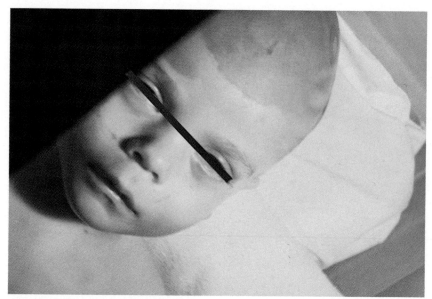

Fractured skull and subdural bleeding.

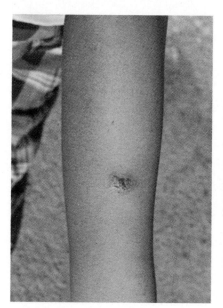

Cigarette burn.

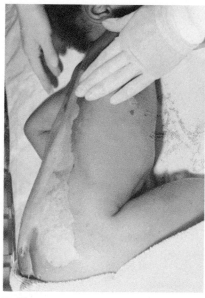

Boiling water poured over child's back.

cooperate with law enforcement, coroner-medical examiners, other official agencies and professionals to protect the health and safety of citizens.

References
1. California Department of Justice, Office of the Attorney General: *Child Abuse Information Pamphlet No. 8.* Revised, October 1978.
2. Schwartz, S., Woolridge, E., and Stege, D.: "The Oral Manifestations and Legal Aspects of Child Abuse." *JADA.* Vol. 95, No. 3, p. 586. September 1977.

Reprint requests to:
  Norman Sperber, DDS
  3737 Moraga Avenue
  Suite A302
  San Diego, CA 92117

Chapter 14

Child Sexual Abuse:
What Happens Next?

by Lucy Berliner
Sexual Assault Center Harborview Medical Center Seattle, Washington

The sexually abused child is not only a victim of sexual exploitation but of societal attitudes which tend to disbelieve or blame the child. She may be traumatized by the reactions of those she turns to for help. It is imperative that the goal of intervention be to focus on the needs of the child by protecting her from further abuse and minimizing the emotional trauma. The victim of sexual abuse is usually a girl who is assaulted nonviolently by an adult male she knows. In one-fourth of the cases, the offender is a family member, and the abuse may continue over a period of years. The victim of an isolated incident committed by a stranger will have the least emotional trauma, while an extremely violent or long term abuse situation may engender severe psychological disturbance.

Victim services should be offered on a 24 hour basis to provide acute medical care and crisis counseling. Although most children are not injured, medical examination is necessary to screen for venereal disease, collect medico-legal evidence and to reassure the parent and child that there has been no permanent injury. Crisis intervention counseling can help the parent cope with the immediate situation, provide information about the criminal justice system, and assist them in decision making.

Following disclosure of the sexual abuse, young children may exhibit behavioral disturbance. The most often reported symptoms are: sleep disturbances; nightmares, irritability and crankiness, excessive dependence on the parent; regressive behavior such as bedwetting and thumbsucking; and fearfulness. These are normal symptoms of emotional distress and will usually improve rapidly. Parents also experience emotional trauma upon learning of the sexual assault. Many parents will have feelings of guilt for failing to protect the child and of anger at the assailant. If the offender is someone known or trusted by the family, it may be difficult for the parent to believe the child or to resolve their ambivalent feelings.

Crisis intervention counseling is effective in providing immediate and intensive intervention for children and families. The families are instructed that the child's emotional health may be determined by the reaction of the parents. In order to resolve the emotional trauma and return the child to normal functioning, the parents must believe the child and never blame the child. If the parents can respond in a supportive but matter-of-fact fashion, the child may integrate the abuse as an unpleasant childhood experience which will not permanently affect her development. The parents will need to alleviate their personal distress without further exacerbating the situation.

When abuse is long term and involves a family member, usually the father, the problems are more complex and require extensive intervention. There is a crisis when the incest is disclosed and crisis intervention counseling as well as long term therapy is indicated. In this case the protection of the child becomes paramount and the offender must not have access to the child. The emotional disturbance of the victim and the nonoffending parent often reflects the pathological dynamics which have developed within the family. The adolescent victim may display guilt, depression, suicidal ideation, suppression of affect or quasi-delinquent behavior. The nonoffending parent also experiences disruption of normal functioning.

Therapeutic intervention alone is not sufficient to protect the victim of child sexual abuse. It is often necessary to involve the child protective services and the criminal justice system. The sex offender will rarely seek treatment voluntarily, and usually will repeat the behavior. In order to insure that he receives treatment for his sexual behavior disorder, the leverage of criminal prosecution may be used. Unfortunately, prosecution may be difficult because there is rarely any corroborating evidence, and the child's testimony is the only source of information. The demands of the criminal justice system may further traumatize the child because there is little recognition of the special needs of the child victim-witness. Efforts should be made to actively intervene on the child's behalf to minimize unnecessary interviews, to be present during questioning, to explain legal proceedings and terminology to the victim and family, and to interpret the child's needs to criminal justice system personnel.

Advocacy with the criminal justice system and other social agencies is an essential component of victim services. The requirements of these agencies often conflict with the goal of returning the child to normal functioning as soon as possible, but if criminal justice system personnel are adequately trained in the area of child sexual abuse and modify or minimize the most difficult aspects of being a victim-witness, the child can often handle the experience of criminal prosecution. Crisis intervention and advocacy are the primary aspects of immediate intervention. Long term therapy is indicated when the child or parent suffer severe psychological disturbance. Fortunately, this is not necessary in most cases if the child's needs are the primary concern of all who become involved.

What If Your Child Tells You She, or He Has Been Sexually Molested?

Be aware that:

1. Children are usually molested by people they know—often a relative or friend of the family.
2. Children are usually not violently attacked or hurt physically during a sexual assault.
3. Children very seldom lie about such a serious matter.
4. Not all children are able to tell parents directly that they have been molested. Changes in behavior, reluctance to be with a certain person or go to a certain place may be signals that something has happened.

What to do immediately:

1. Go with the child to a private place. Ask the child to tell you what happened in her/his own words, and listen, carefully.
2. Tell her/him she/he did well to tell you, that you are very sorry this happened, and that you will protect her/him from further molestation.
3. If you suspect your child has an injury, contact your regular physician or hospital of choice.
4. You may call the police immediately and a uniformed officer will come to your house to take an initial report.
5. You may call the County Probation Department or County Department of Public Welfare.

Helping your child following the assault:

1. Continue to believe your child and do not blame your child for what happened.
2. Consult with your physician or the Sexual Assault Center regarding need for medical examination.
3. Instruct your child to tell you immediately if the offender attempts sexual molestation in the future.
4. Give your child reassurance and support that she/he is okay.
5. Respond to questions or feelings your child expresses about the molestation with a calm, matter-of-fact attitude but do not pressure your child to talk about it.
6. Respect privacy of child by not telling a lot of people or letting other people question her/him.
7. Try to follow regular routine around the home (expect usual chores, bedtimes, rules).
8. Inform brothers/sisters that something has happened to the child but that it is being taken care of. Do not give details.
9. Take the time to talk it over privately with someone you trust—your spouse, a friend, a relative, a counselor. Express your feelings. Do not discuss the situation in front of your child/children.

The most common immediate problems of sexually molested children are:

1. Sleep disturbances (nightmares, fear of going to bed, wanting light on, waking up during night, fear of sleeping alone).
2. Loss of appetite.
3. Irritability, crankiness, short-tempered behavior.
4. Bedwetting.
5. Needing more reassurance than usual, clinging to parent.
6. Changes in behavior at school or in relating to friends.
7. Fears.
8. Behaving as a younger child (regression).

These are normal signs of upset. Your child may have some of these problems or none at all. They usually last a couple of weeks. Try to notice all changes in usual behavior, and discuss with your counselor.

No one knows for sure about long-term emotional effects, but we believe that if the situation is handled in a direct and sensitive way at the time it is revealed, your child need not suffer from the assault.

Some Data on Sexual Abuse of Children

I. Definition:
The sexual exploitation of a child who is not developmentally capable of understanding and resisting the contact or who may be psychologically and socially dependent upon the offender.

II.

A. General Characteristics:
Sex of child: 93 percent female; 7 percent male.
Age of child: 2 years to 18 years.
Relationship of offender: 75 percent known; 25 percent stranger.
Sex of offender: 99 percent male; 1 percent female.
Non-violent: 3 percent injuries.

B. Incest
Sex of child: 95 percent female; 5 percent male.
Age at onset: 81 percent 12 years or younger; 19 percent over 12
Duration: 13 percent one incident; 20 percent 0 to 6 months; 67 percent 1 to 14 years.
Relationship of assailant: 75 percent father/stepfather; 7 percent mother's live-in boyfriend; 18 percent uncles, grandfathers, brothers, grandmother.
Sex of Offender: 99 percent male; 1 percent female.

III. Myths
A. Children lie/fantasize about sexual contact with adults.
B. Children enjoy, provoke, or are partially responsible for sexual contact with adults.
C. (Incest) Mother colludes in incestuous relationship.
D. Non-violent sexual abuse is not emotionally traumatic.

IV. Effects
A. Signs of distress exhibited through behavior changes; correlated with parental reaction.
B. Medical care.
C. Advocacy: Child Protective Service, criminal justice system, other social agencies.
D. Ongoing counseling: individual, family.
E. Consultation.

Chapter 15

Preliminary Investigation of the Sexual Exploitation/Abuse of Children by Chickenhawks and Child Molesters

PART I

The exploitation and abuse of children by anyone is a serious crime, one that receives the fullest measure of attention from law enforcement personnel. Recent studies and available information indicate an increase in the scope of sexual exploitation and abuse of children. This type of crime can occur anywhere and suspects may be rich or poor, ignorant or well-educated, married or single. They can come from any sector of society.

In the course of their duties, officers may encounter cases of sexual exploitation/abuse and should be prepared to take appropriate action. In order to do so, there is a need for officers to develop the skills and acquire the knowledge necessary to recognize these situations where they exist and to conduct a thorough preliminary investigation, when so directed. This provides a follow-up investigator a solid base on which to build a case.

This series of bulletins will provide information on those laws applicable to sexual exploitation/abuse of children. Profiles of potential victims and suspects will be presented to aid in recognition. Additionally, the function of the Sexually Exploited Child Unit (SECU) will be explained. Juvenile Division generally will handle these investigations, nevertheless, the field officer should know how to proceed when confronted by a situation in which a child is the victim of sexual abuse or exploitation.

The Law

There are several laws which define and prohibit conduct which may subject children to sexual exploitation. In addition, the law grants law enforcement specific authority to deal with situations which involve these offenses. These laws will be briefly described and only the more common offenses will be covered.

Children who become the victims of sex-related offenses may become wards of the juvenile court under the provisions of 300 W.I.C.

"300 W.I.C. Dependent Children—Jurisdiction

Any persons under the age of 18 years who comes within any of the following descriptions is within the jurisdiction of the Juvenile Court which may adjudge such person to be a dependent child of the court:

300(d) W.I.C. Whose home is an unfit place for him by reason of neglect, cruelty, depravity, physical abuse of either or both parents, or of his guardian or other person in whose custody or care he is:"

NOTE: This section is divided into four (4) booking/filing categories for statistical purposes.

"300(d) W.I.C. (Physical Abuse)
300(d) W.I.C. (Sexual Molestation)
300(d) W.I.C. (Unfit Home)
300(d) W.I.C. (Endangering)"

Law enforcement personnel are empowered to take action to protect a juvenile victim under the provisions of Section 305 W.I.C., Legal Authority for Arrest.

Essentially, 305 W.I.C. limits the authority of officers not equipped with a warrant to three particular situations. Such situations are those involving persons under the age of 18 years who fit the description of a minor under 300 W.I.C., dependent children of the court (including those who violate orders of the juvenile court) or any person under 18 years found in a public place, sick or injured, and in need of care.

There are situations in which an officer may encounter both juvenile offenders as well as juvenile victims. When the conduct of a juvenile consists of sexually-oriented offensive acts, the subject may come within the purview of 601 or 602 W.I.C. In such situations, officers should be guided by the advice of the Area Juvenile Coordinator or Juvenile Division.

The following Penal Code sections include those offenses which officers may frequently encounter in sexual exploitation/molestation cases. These sections will be listed only to serve as a quick reference and guide for officers.

261.5 P.C.	Unlawful sexual intercourse (Misd/Felony)
266(i) P.C.	Pandering (Felony)
272 P.C.	Contributing to delinquency of a minor (Misdemeanor)
273(a) P.C.	Willful cruelty toward child; endangering life, limb, or health.
	273(a) (1) P.C. (Felony)
	273(a) (2) P.C. (Misdemeanor)
286 P.C.	Sodomy with a minor (Felony)
288 P.C.	Crimes against children (Felony)
288(a) P.C.	Oral copulation with a minor (Felony)
311.2 P.C.	Sale or distribution of obscene matter (Misdemeanor)
311.4 P.C.	Hiring, employing, etc., a minor for sale or distribution of obscene matter.
	311.4(a) (Misdemeanor)
	311.4(b) (Felony)
647(a) P.C.	Annoying or molesting children (Misdemeanor)

The sections indicated above are not all inclusive. A complete description can be obtained from the Penal Code. The application of the above described offenses under current case law can be obtained from the Area Juvenile Coordinator, Juvenile Division, or the Legal Systems Section of Planning and Research Division.

Although officers may be familiar with the elements of some of the above described crimes, an effort should be made to become familiar with the elements of all those mentioned.

Recognition of Victims and Suspects

Officers should become familiar with the people who frequent locations where juveniles congregate. The frequent appearance of adults may indicate that the location is a meeting place or a pick-up point.

Officers should also be familiar with the terms which are used to refer to victims and suspects. This will aid in recognition.

Pedophile (ped-a-file): One with a sex perversion in which children are the preferred sexual objeet.

Child Molester: An adult male or female who seeks sexual gratification from young girls.

Chickenhawk: An adult male or female who seeks sexual gratification from young boys.

Chicken: A young boy under the age of 18 years.

A chickenhawk has a sexual preference limited to boys of a certain age range which may not span more than three years, i.e., boys nine, ten, and eleven years. A 12-year-old boy would not be sexually stimulating to this particular chickenhawk. The child molester has a broader sexual preference age range. The age preference may cover as much as a ten year span.

Child molesters and chickenhawks have a genuine interest in children. Most of these individuals have no children of their own. Because of their sexual preference, they must continually seek out new children. Officers should be aware that the chickenhawk or child molester is often the child's best friend. The sexually exploited child is seduced through attention and affection. The relationship between the victim and suspect may be so close as to give the impression of a parent-child relationship. The victim may, in fact, believe that nothing is wrong with what the chickenhawk or child molester does. Officers should also be aware that there are usually numerous victims involved.

There are several factors which can aid officers in identifying victims and suspects. Some of these factors may be readily apparent and others may become known only after an interview.

The victims of child molesters and chickenhawks usually are:

a. in the 8–16 age bracket;
b. unsupervised and may be runaways.
c. from an unstable home environment with poor family ties and perhaps one parent absent.
d. underachievers at home and at school.
e. from low or average income families.
f. subject to abrupt changes in moods, attitude and behaviors.
g. without strong moral or religious values.
h. not necessarily delinquent.
i. seeking attention, praise, rewards, and approval.

j. in possession of more money than normal, new toys, new clothes, etc. (rewards from the child molester or chicken-hawk).

k. found at recreation areas, theatres, and other juvenile hang-outs where they may spend more than the normal amount of time.

l. in the company of adults with whom they spend inordinate amounts of time.

m. withdrawn from family and peer groups and may form new peer groups.

The profile of a child molester/chickenhawk suspect would generally include the following:

a. more often a middle-age male.

b. relates far better to children than to adults.

c. usually unmarried but may have a "protective marriage."

d. associated with few adults except other pediphiles;

e. usually has an identifiable sexual preference in regard to children and will frequent locations that cater to them.

f. may seek employment and/or volunteer programs involving children of his sexual preference;

g. sexually pursues children by
   1. eye contact, and
   2. furtive glances, or
   3. staring at the genital area of a prospective victim;

h. pays more than a normal amount of attention to a child in his company (doting);

i. usually photographs the victims;

j. collects child pornography and uses it for self-gratification as well as for lowering the inhibition of victims;

k. may possess and use narcotics to lower the inhibitions of victims;

l. may have a genuine interest in children;

m. is usually intelligent enough to recognize his personal problem and to understand the severity of it;

n. may go to great lengths to conceal the illicit activity;

o. often rationalizes any involvement, emphasizing the positive impact upon the victim and repressing the harm committed;

p. often portrays the child as the sexual aggressor;

q. talks about the child in the same manner as one would talk about an adult lover or spouse;

r. often was molested at an early age, and

s. is usually non-violent and has few problems with the law.

Sexually Exploited Child Unit (SECU)

The Sexually Exploited Child Unit is within the Child Protection Section, Juvenile Division. This unit will meet the growing need for the investigative expertise in cases of children. SECU investigators provide assistance to Area investigators with complex sexual abuse/exploitation cases involving children. The normal working hours for the members of this unit are 0830–1700 (extension 2883), however, they are on 24 hour call, seven days a week. Officers who require the expertise of SECU during off hours should call IHD, extension 2504, and request the on-call SECU investigator.

Conclusion

Part 1 of this series has focused upon the problem of the sexual exploitation of children. The laws which restrict this activity were briefly covered and information was provided to aid officers in the identification of victims, suspects, and places where they meet. The duties of the Sexually Exploited Child Unit were briefly explained to inform officers of whom they should contact for assistance and investigative expertise. Part II will present information to aid field officers who become involved in the investigation of sexual exploitation/abuse cases.

PART II

In Part I of this series of bulletins, the problem of sexual exploitation/abuse of children was discussed. The laws which are most commonly involved in offenses of this kind were enumerated. Profiles were provided of "the victim" and "the suspect" as an identification aid to officers. In Part II additional information will be provided to assist officers involved in the initial or preliminary phase of an investigation.

Victim Interview

An officer who has occasion to interview a victim should keep in mind the fact that this particular victim is an emotionally confused individual. Most victims are "willing victims" in spite of the fact that they have known lies, misuse and abuse at the hands of the molester or chickenhawk. Nevertheless, the chickenhawk and molester are generally the only individuals who have ever given a victim affection and attention. Consequently, the victim has no reason to expect any better treatment from a police officer than that received from any other adult. An officer must establish and maintain rapport with the victim. Only then will the victim trust an officer.

An officer can acquire the trust of a victim by exhibiting the following characteristics:

    a. Be attentive (really listen to the victim),
    b. Be honest,
    c. Be patient (it can take hours to establish the trust necessary to reveal the details of sexual activities),
    d. Be understanding (particularly of the underlying factors of a victim's involvement in sexual exploitation),
    e. Show genuine concern.

During any interview at least two officers should be present. This is particularly the case when interviewing a child who has been the victim of a sex crime. In some events, depending on the age and sex of the victim, a female officer should also be involved in the interview. This affords investigating officers protection against false allegations of sexual misconduct by a victim who subsequently becomes uncooperative.

As soon as the officer has established the rapport necessary, the course of the interview should be directed to include the specifics of the case under investigation. Have the victim identify the suspect(s) as well as possible. Anything unique or unusual about the suspect's personal clothing, vehicle or residence should be noted. Even seemingly trivial information can strengthen a case when it is later corroborated. Following this, questions should be asked about the specific acts committed by the suspect upon the victim and those which the victim was induced to commit upon the suspect. Officers should determine what inducement or persuasion the suspect employed, to gain the victim's recall. Why the victim clearly recalls one aspect of involvement as opposed to another is a question that will arise in court and may be pertinent to the prosecution. This should be brought out and covered in the officer's report.

Many child molesters/chickenhawks employ pornography and/ or narcotics not only for their self gratification, but also to lower the inhibitions of their victims. If the suspect did use one or both of these, have the victim describe the manner in which it was used and where on the premise or in the vehicle it (pornography/narcotics) was kept. Victims should be asked whether or not they were photographed and whether they had seen photos of other children who might be victims. Include this information in all reports to describe the suspects' or arrestees' M.O. This information will be coded and entered into the Department's automated systems for investigative and statistical purposes.

Interrogation of Suspects

The interrogation of adult suspects should be handled tactfully to elicit their cooperation. Child molesters and chickenhawks are well aware of the low esteem in which society holds them. They are also aware of the consequences of going to prison under a child molesting conviction. For this reason, they fear going to prison and generally react to the hard approach by total withdrawal, completely denying all allegations. However, when these suspects are approached with the understanding that they have an emotional problem which can be treated, they become more cooperative in interview situations. Remember that many child molesters/chickenhawks are individuals who had similar experiences in their youth. Once an officer gains their confidence, they may open up and talk about the incident.

Chickenhawks/child molesters usually associate with other pedophiles and, consequently, can provide information on other sexual exploitation activity.

Reporting Specifics

Most officers are conscientious about including in their reports the elements of the crime, chronologically relating all those events which contributed to probable cause, and led to a good arrest. In sexually exploitative/abuse crimes against children there is often much evidence not collected and, consequently, not reported. This evidence is often essential to show intent. It is also vital for statistics to discover M.O.'s as well as the relationship between certain types of crimes and particular items of evidence. Pornography, both that which is legal as well as that which is illicit, is often used by suspects in these crimes to lower a victim's inhibition and to persuade a victim to participate in the desired sexual act. Investigators have discovered through their investigations and through interviews with child molesters, chickenhawks, and their victims that pornography and drugs are commonly used to gain a victim's compliance.

When officers receive information for a crime report or any related report that narcotics or pornography was present at the scene of or used in the commission of any sex crime, this information should be included in the narrative section of the report. When collecting evidence at the scene of a sex crime or in any other place in which an officer had a legal right to collect evidence, all pornographic material, even that which is legitimately sold at newsstands, should be booked into evidence and noted on the appropriate reports.

Search Warrants and Informants

The use of search warrants and informants with regard to exploitation/molestation cases are generally beyond any investigative action a field officer may take. However, for the benefit of those officers who may become involved in a follow-up investigation, certain general guidelines will be presented.

The preparation of a search warrant will require reliable information that such activity is taking place. The statements of victims should be corroborated. Other victims and suspects should be identified and described as well. When executing a search warrant extensive photographs should be taken of the location, interior furnishings, and particularly, anything which may corroborate the victim's statements.

When an officer uses an informant, the reliability of the informant should be established. Victims and suspects should be identified. Locations at which chickenhawks and child molesters and their victims meet and, if possible, the locations where the sexual activity takes place should be identified. An informant can be used to verify the statements of victims, suspects, and witnesses. When dealing with an informant, the nature of information should be detailed and explicit as possible. Subsequent confirmation of this information will lend greater weight to the testimony of the informant. Even in the event an informant does not testify in court, confirming information given by the informant to officers strengthens the informant's reliability for future cases. Informants may or may not be involved in the type of activity under investigation. Thought should be given to an informant's motivation as well as how the informant came to possess the information provided to the officers.

Conclusion

Officers should be aware that the problem exists and that field officers too can perform a vital role in repressing this activity. The key to repressing this activity is a knowledge of the information brought out in this series of bulletins.

Chapter 16

Incest

by Carolyn F. Bailey
Sergeant, St. Paul Police Department St. Paul, Minnesota

Although the actual extent of incest cannot be documented, due to limited available statistics and non-reporting, many police departments are suddenly being confronted with increasing complaints of sexual abuse within the family. Reports received in Ramsey County, Minnesota, increased 300 percent in a one-year period, and yet many researchers feel known cases are still just the "tip of the iceberg." Unlike aggravated rape, which has shown greater concentration in larger cities, *incest permeates the rural as well as the urban communities.* With limited knowledge and training, the police officer is increasingly expected to investigate and resolve the most difficult, frustrating, and challenging of all offences: incest.

Most states now have laws that require reporting to authorities of physical and sexual abuse to children by a parent, guardian or other person responsible for the child's care. Criminal statutes generally describe "incest" as sexual intercourse between relatives nearer than first cousins with the knowledge of the relationship. For investigative purposes, the broader range of "sexual abuse" cases are included because investigative techniques are similar. There may not be actual intercourse but sodomy or other molesting involved in the sexual abuse; and although there may be no blood relationship, one views the relationship as incestuous because the offender is serving as a parent, such as a stepfather or mother's boy friend who is living in the home.[1]

Since father-daughter sexual abuse cases are the most often reported to police, for simplicity we will refer to the offender as he and victim/child as she, but it should be emphasized that there are many male children who are victims of sexual abuse and some female adults who are the perpetrators. The possibility that male children may also

Acknowledgment is made to Carolyn F. Bailey and Seattle Sexual Assault Center for their help in compiling this information.

1. "Mars Man"—Male assuming the role of spouse.

be involved should be paramount in the investigator's consideration of such cases. Also, during the investigation of father-daughter incest cases, it frequently has developed that brother-sister (or even other relatives) incest is also involved.

Probably more than any other type of offense, the incest investigation must be initiated and completed as quickly as possible after the report is brought to the attention of outside authorities. It is urgent that each family member be carefully questioned immediately after they are aware of the investigation and that this be documented because attitudes often change quickly and evidence is lost.

Assessing and Questioning

If the reporting source is other than the victim, as much detailed information as is possible should be obtained before the initial contact with the victim. How did the reporter obtain the information? Was it direct observation, suspicion or verbal complaints from a family member? Carefully prepared background information greatly facilitates the questioning of the victim.

The child who is the victim should be interviewed first before contacting any other family members. If the parents are aware the child is to be questioned, they may interfere and attempt to prevent the report. This is an extremely difficult interview, upon which the entire outcome of the investigation is based. The victim must be supported, reassured that she is not to blame, and must trust that the results of providing the report will be an improved lifestyle or she will not provide complete information.

If the victim herself has initiated the report, this is an advantage to the investigator because the child has already decided she can no longer tolerate the incest situation and desires a change. If the incest is initially reported by a social worker, it frequently is most effective to have the social worker bring the child in for a statement because the worker may already have a relationship with the child and the child may feel more comfortable. When the child has sought help, the child's primary concern often is finding a place to live. She frequently doesn't seem to care where she is to live as long as it is not with her father (or the incestuous relative). However, if the victim is asked what she would like more than anything else in the world, she usually will respond, "To be home with my mother, brothers, and sisters without my father there." Because of the need to protect the child, frequently she must be moved away from her family rather than the offender. This can later be seen as "punishment" and can further increase the child's feelings of guilt and responsibility for what has happened. Where it is possible, the offender should be removed rather than the child, but in cases where the offender is likely to bail out of jail and become violent, for example, it may be too great a risk to allow the child to remain in her own home. A police protective hold on the child is frequently utilized in these cases (most states have legal provisions). Placement of a child outside her home should be made on the basis of the immediate physical threat to the child of repeated sexual abuse and physical violence, the child's own fear and attitude, including her refusal to return home, and the need to prevent coercion of the child by one or both parents.

The child may be reluctant to tell her mother about the incest because she is ashamed and feels her mother is "too weak" to deal with the reality of incest (and frequently she is).

In questioning, determine from the child:

1. The most recent incident of incest, including a detailed sequence of events and the specific act itself.
2. The duration of offenses, including the initial contact, the nature and frequency of the molestings, and any specific dates available. A specific date of offense must be determined if prosecution is to be considered.
3. Are there any possible witnesses? This could be someone who merely came home early and felt it suspicious that the victim and offender were in the bedroom alone with the door closed, someone who heard the victim crying or someone who actually saw the offense. Friends of the victim, babysitters, and other relatives are often surprising witnesses or additional victims.
4. Who has the child told about the offense? A person whom the victim may have told immediately after the offense can be an excellent corroborating witness. Also, if the child told her mother it is significant to know whether the mother took action to protect her child, if she chose to ignore her, did not believe her or just hoped it wouldn't happen again.

A medical examination of the child may be indicated if intercourse is reported. Although incest is seldom reported immediately after the offense when sperm may be present, the medical examination may demonstrate the extent of penetration and provide treatment for possible injuries and venereal disease (uncommon among these victims). This examination is especially traumatic for the incest victim and should be tactfully explained to the child.

The parents of the victim should never be questioned together. The presence of the husband or wife can greatly limit or distort the information obtained. It is usually easier to maintain control of the case and less likely to create an immediate crisis if the mother can be questioned alone before the incestuous father is aware the complaint has been made. Although the mother frequently expresses surprise about the incest, she may later relate earlier suspicions. These should be noted because they may become relevant. Subtle comments made by the mother may indicate her previous denial of the incest. The nature and/or change in the mother's relationship with her husband may also be significant. The mother is usually receptive to the child's temporary removal from the home, although her willingness seems to decrease as the age of the child decreases. Unless she has actually witnessed the incest and summoned the police to the scene of the offense, the mother is frequently reluctant to separate from her husband, and, if she does, she often will reunite with him. The mothers in these cases should be considered extremely unreliable during the entire investigation. Even if she initially accepts the offense as valid, she may later deny it or blame the child. She is frequently very protective of her husband and feels dependent on him. If the mother can provide corroborating evidence, such as witnessing the offense, a written statement should be obtained immediately because she may later refuse to provide any information. This may be especially true if she has been married previously and this involves her second or third husband.

If it is explained to the mother that the officer is aware that this is a very difficult situation for her, that there will be professionals to help her and the family, and that the police responsibility is to assure the child's safety, the mother may be more likely to be cooperative. She may retaliate if the officer is quick to condemn her husband's actions rather than seek facts and explanations. It is important to convey to the mother the validity of the offense rather than argue about this because it is easier emotionally for the mother to deny the offense occurred. The investigation proceeds more smoothly and it is far easier for the child if the mother is able to accept the facts of the offense.

Physical evidence, such as pornographic magazines, contraceptives, etc., should be obtained as quickly as possible and may be available through the mother at the time of the initial notification.

Questioning of the father can be most effective in the police station. Frequently the father will come in voluntarily if asked and if immediate arrest is not indicated. An emotional approach in questioning the incestuous father is frequently effective, because the father often will express guilt about the incest and relief that the "secret" is out. Encouraging the father to explain his own difficulties in childhood, marriage, sex, etc., allows him an opportunity to "save face." If you become aware that he is one of the incestuous fathers who appear to feel that sexual abuse is appropriate, justified (as with certain religious arguments), and acceptable, then a matter-of-fact, no-big-deal approach might be effective. If the father admits the sexual abuse, an attempt should be made to obtain specific information about each incident, especially where dates may be available. Details, such as the exchange of money, which corroborate the child's account, lend further credibility to the complaint.

Research Findings

Utilize knowledge of the incestuous families during the investigation. Research generally indicates:

- The child reporting the sexual abuse is usually telling the truth.
- The oldest daughter is most frequently the first victim.
- Incest will perpetuate and permeate other victims unless there is effective intervention (transference syndrome).
- The incestuous father is frequently chemically dependent (most often alcoholic and physically violent to most family members.

The investigation should be referred to the local child protection agency that can provide considerable assistance during the investigation and services to the family. Many prosecution cases are successful as a result of the ongoing support provided to the witnesses by the social service agencies.

Conclusion

There has been a tendency to over-react to incest as a nameless sexual evil with disastrous effects. It is important to respond to the child who has been the victim of sexual abuse with warmth, objectivity, and acceptance, so that the child is not bound up in sexual fear and the entire process which follows is not demoralizing and ineffective.

We can help the child recognize the fact that sex is simply a part of life, one of the ways in which people relate to one another. It has the potential for either good or bad. If we are irrational about sex, it is not because sex is an irrational force but because we choose to be irrational. We dare not choose to be irrational at a time when a child comes to us in serious need of common sense and good judgment.

Chapter 17

Incest: The Victim and the Family

Despite individual differences among them, we believe that incestuous families can be described by certain personality traits, behaviors, and family interaction patterns which tend to characterize them. In this chapter we will attempt to describe the personal characteristics and behaviors of incest victims and their families which we have found helpful in identifying them. Our practice had been generally limited to girls, but, in those instances of father-son incest is by no means rare, as was once thought, but we do not yet have the knowledge to comment on its similarities to more commonly reported forms of family sexual abuse.

We stress two notes of caution. First, the presence of a pattern of characteristics in the child, the child's parents, and the family system can alert us to the likelihood of sexual abuse in that family. Reliance on single behavior signs is of little value. Although one particular behavior may arouse our suspicions and appropriately result in our inquiring whether incest is present, often a problem other than sexual abuse may account for the behavior. Secondly, incest is ultimately identified by receiving a report. The actual means of identification is sensitive questioning (or sometimes receptive listening) by someone the reporting person trusts to help him or her. The child, a parent, or a concerned other tells us that incest is present. The patterns of characteristics and behaviors that we will discuss in this section are only aids to identification that alert us to inquire.

Characteristics of the Victim

Data were collected in Ramsey County, Minnesota, between 1970 and 1976, which tell us something about the typical incest victim. The oldest girl was almost always the first victim, but in more than half of these families, younger sisters were also abused and concurrent brother-sister incest was frequent. On the average, incest began at about the age of ten but was not reported for two years. Actual intercourse occurred in over half the cases. Other forms of sexual abuse included oral-genital and anal contact, penetration with objects, touching of breasts and genital area, and forcing the child to masturbate and perform fellatio on the abuser.

Clinical experience with these children and others reveal a number of common personal characteristics. A hallmark of these youngsters is pervasive low self-esteem. Their sexual experiences in the family have left them a reservoir of shame and guilt. Their poor self-concepts may be manifested in depression, withdrawal, and/or self-destructive acting out.

Incest victims may exhibit a misleading facade of sophistication and maturity. Their pseudo-maturity masks an underlying childlike personality. At home they typically have heavy housekeeping and child care responsibilities, sometimes to the point of reversing roles with their mothers. Because they have never been permitted a normal childhood, they have overwhelming, unmet dependency needs. Abused by their fathers and frequently neglected by their mothers, yet dependent on them for care and affection, these children experience intense ambivalence toward both parents.

Incest victims can appear to be very disturbed, sometimes to the point of psychosis, but, in our experience, occasional psychotic behavior is often hysterical in origin rather than schizophrenic. By hysterical we mean the child exhibits such pre-psychotic personality characteristics as denial, somatization, self-dramatization and seductiveness.

Case #1. Fourteen-year-old Judy had been in treatment approximately nine months when she began to experience episodes of hallucinations and delusions. These episodes, which lasted several hours each time, consisted of her hallucinating the image of her father approaching her sexually and her believing that her foster mother was conspiring with unspecified others to kill her. She expressed terror during the episodes but was totally amnesic of them afterwards. Prior to the development of these psychotic symptoms, Judy had presented herself as cheerful and friendly. She denied any anger toward family members, three of whom had abused her. Early in foster placement she had made dramatic suicide threats and gestures which required all-night vigils on the part of her foster mother. She complained of severe headaches and stomach pains for which no physical basis could be discovered.

As mentioned earlier, one characteristic of incest victims is self-destructive acting out. While suicide attempts may bring them to hospital emergency rooms, their behavior more frequently brings them to the attention of police and juvenile corrections personnel. Running away and truancy are common, as are chemical dependency and drug abuse. In one survey of runaways, sexual abuse was listed as one of three primary reasons why children chose to leave home (*Runaways Newsletter,* 1975). James (1975) reported that more than 50 percent of the female children placed in one reformatory in Maine had been molested prior to commitment. Siverson, a family therapist who has treated 500 cases of adolescent chemical dependency, found that of these, 70 percent has experienced some form of family sexual abuse (*Ms. Magazine,* 1977).

> Case #2: In her appearance and manner, sixteen-year-old
> Shirley blended the features of a kittenish sexuality with those
> of a plaintive, lost child. She first came to the attention of
> juvenile authorities at the age of 14 for repeated truancy and
> running away from home. Placed in a foster home, Shirley
> became pregnant by her foster brother, necessitating
> replacement in a residential treatment facility. Her pregnancy
> was terminated and Shirley did well in the institutional setting
> with its structure and limits. After release from this setting,
> however, Shirley began heavy use of alcohol and established
> relationships with a succession of physically abusive boyfriends
> who were also engaged in criminal behavior.

Problematic sexual behavior and attitudes are invariably a legacy of sexual abuse, typified by an exaggerated attitude toward sex. Victims may manifest either of two extremes—aversion to sex or promiscuity. The girl who fears or hates men and sex is often more easily identified and understood than the victim who becomes promiscuous.

A promiscuous or seductive child is often the result, but never the cause, of incest. A Twin Cities' study of juvenile prostitution (Enablers, 1978) revealed that more than one third of these children had been sexually abused by members of their families. Such children have learned only one way to gain affection from men. Desperately needy, they know no alternative to presenting themselves to be used, and many seem to court disrespect in a self-destructive manner. Incestuous fathers often justify their own sexual behavior with their daughters as a way of "keeping them off the streets" or minimize the behavior with statements such as "she asked for it—she's a tramp." We suspect that promiscuous behavior in these girls may also serve a retaliatory function by acting out their father's fears and prophecies.

Children seldom demonstrate adult forms of depression before the age of 16. Rather, their depression appears in the form of depressive equivalents, such as acting out behavior. For purposes of identification, we have separated running away, truancy, drug abuse, and promiscuity from depression and withdrawal. For purposes of understanding these children, however, all these symptoms are best seen as manifestations of the same depressive process. Incest victims are almost always depressed.

Identification of Sexual Abuse in Medical Setting

Children and adolescents who are victims of sexual abuse may present to their physician with very subtle complaints.[1] The physician needs to be aware that incest does occur in all levels of society and that lack of recognition and under-reporting is the rule.

Sexual abuse of children perhaps occurs as commonly as physical child abuse. A pediatrician may provide care for a family for years without knowing that incest is occurring. The physician, therefore, must be aware of the characteristics of the victim and the family described here and must learn to recognize the clues pointing to the existence of incest.

A physician may become suspicious because he/she notes that the young child or adolescent he/she is examining has an ususual or strange affect. The patient may be extremely distrustful of the medical examination, want to know exactly what the doctor is going to do to his/her body and not wanting to be touched. As part of the symptom complex of the victim's depression and low self-esteem, the child may present with somatic complaints such as fatigue, headache or stomachache, or may even present with hysterical type signs and symptoms such as hysterical paralysis, or mimicking Guillain Barre Syndrome (Kempe, 1978). The recent onset of rebellious or acting out behavior, poor school attendance and lowered school performance may also be clues to his depression. Younger children who are being sexually abused may just react with excessive fear and clinging behavior or may demonstrate some form of regression in their development. The onset of day or nighttime bedwetting may also be a clue. Older adolescent girls, who

1. *"Present" means to show personal body areas, usually the genital areas.*

114

wet either during the day or at night, should be considered as incest victims. Children who are noted to be seductive or are unusually preoccupied with sex and are frequently heard discussing sexual anatomy and intercourse at a time when their peer group is much more inhibited in these discussions are suspect as victims, as are children who have explicit understanding of intercourse, erection and ejaculation. The following cases demonstrate some of these characteristics of incest victims.

> Case #3. A twelve-year-old girl, not aware that her older sister had also been involved with their father for several years, presented with the chief complaint of "sweaty hands" and did literally have a massive amount of perspiration almost dripping from her fingers. Her older sister, four years earlier, had suddenly become rebellious, ignoring any curfew that the family would set for her. At one time she chased the father around the house with a butcher knife and was sent to live with the grandmother in another city. This went unrecognized by medical and welfare authorities until it came out as part of the investigation of the twelve-year-old victim. On multiple occasions the mother brought her daughters to their pediatrician, seeking help for these behavior and somatic problems.

> Case #4. A three-year-old boy was brought to the pediatrician by his parents, complaining that he had begun to wet both day and night, and was masturbating excessively even to the point of crawling into his bed during the daytime to masturbate under the covers, ending in wetting his bed. When questioned, he stated that his teenage babysitter would lie on top of him and rub his penis. He was observed attempting this behavior with a four-year-old playmate at the babysitters and stated when asked what he was doing that he was "making honey." On gentle questioning of the teenage babysitter, she too was found to have been sexually assaulted within her family at an early age.

Identification of Sexual Abuse in a School Setting

School personnel should keep in mind that it is important to be aware of some of the signs that may indicate that a child is being sexually abused. Some of the most common signs include:

1. Depression
2. Withdrawal, i.e., the child who appears to have few friends.
3. Chemical abuse

4. Truancy and persistent running away behavior
5. Poor self-image which might include inappropriate clothing, cleanliness, etc.
6. Drop in academic performance
7. Lack of involvement in social activities because of self choice or because of over-restrictive demands on the part of the family.
8. Recurrent somatic complaints to the school nurse.

Characteristics of the Family

The typical incestuous family system can best be described as character disordered. Interactions among family members are characterized by acting out behavior and poor impulse control, which serve as substitutes for direct verbal communication. No one talks about what is really going on. This type of family system tends to foster narcissitic, self centered personalities in its members. Given these characteristics, it is not surprising that family violence is a common accompaniment of incest: in 47 percent of the incestuous families seen in Ramsey County, physical abuse of children has occurred; in 39 percent, physical abuse of the wife was reported. Sexual abuse is frequently transmitted from generation to generation. Offenders often were child victims, and current victims may victimize others.

For the sake of simplicity, we have described the family structure of victims of father-daughter incest. It should be kept in mind, however, that the victim may be a male child and the abuser may be a family member other than the father.

Socioeconomic status is of no help to identifying incest. Incest appears to occur at all levels of income and education. Most of the families we have seen present an appearance of respectability. The father has been a good provider and often insists on such things as regular church attendance. Respect for the father is demanded of the children, and once the incest has been exposed, the mother usually resists informing the siblings in order to preserve the father's image of respectability. However, the "secret" of father's sexual deviation is generally a secret only in that the mother is unaware that the children already know and may also be involved.

Ordinarily, the sexually abusive family is united by very strong, though pathological, bonds. Whether a separation occurs voluntarily or involuntarily as the result of community intervention, eventually the family is likely to reunite. These families have been self-contained, socially isolated systems, highly resistant to intervention by outsiders. Effective intervention strategies must be geared to penetrating the system, relaxing the rigid boundaries and allowing input from outside, while accomodating the family's press to ultimately reunite.

Characteristics of the Mother

In our practice, we have observed two relatively distinct personality types among mothers of incest victims. The more common is the dependent individual who reverses roles with her daughter. The child assumes her mother's responsibilities for all family members and takes care of her mother's emotional needs as well. Although this kind of woman seems to abdicate her wifely role, she nonetheless resents her daughter's favored position with her husband. Her feelings for her daughter alternate between jealousy and motherly concern. The women's dependency on her husband requires her to ignore hints and signs and to believe her husband over her daughter when confronted with the fact of incest. This confrontation usually occurs when the daughter tells the mother, sometimes years before it comes to community attention. The mother's denial allows the incest to continue.

Less common is the stronger mother who frequently is working and can be financially independent. This woman takes a strong parenting role and can verbally express her ambivalence toward her daughter and her rage toward her husband, whom she casts out upon learning of the incest.

These differences in personality type may be blurred in the data complied by Ramsey County. One cannot tell from these data whether the high rate of physical abuse by husbands and alcohol abuse among the mothers of incest victims (26%) is primarily associated with the dependent personality type. We suspect that this is the case.

Characteristics of the Father

In 60 percent of the Ramsey County cases, the sexual abuser was the natural father of the child. Thirty-nine percent were stepfathers or other males functioning in the role of a father. Our experience suggests that the psychological impact on the victim does not differ between cases of abuse by natural fathers and abuse by stepfathers of long standing who have become psychological parents to their stepdaughters.

Within the family system, the sexually abusive father is typically overcontrolling and overly restrictive. Many of the fathers we have seen require their teenage daughters to come home immediately after school and forbid their participation in normal recreational activities that would permit interaction with boys of their own age. They maintain their control through excessive discipline, even to the point of physical abuse. Their wives are equally subject to their tyranny. Sometimes they exercise their control by means of special favors granted to the victim. The mother may perceive the victim as spoiled by the father, but his gifts actually serve as bribes to elicit favors and/or to maintain secrecy.

A defining feature of incestuous fathers is their difficulty with impulse control. They frequently believe that they "need" sex and must have it readily available to them at all times. We have documented their poor control of their anger in the statistics on family violence. Other indications of their poor impulse control include a 65 percent rate of alcohol abuse and a 37 percent rate of previous criminal records among these men.

When confronted with their incestuous behavior, the fathers almost always initially deny the accusation. If their denial is not accepted, they may eventually admit the behavior, but project blame for it onto their daughters and their wives. They may admit to some "lesser offense" than that with which they have been charged by the daughter, thereby justifying an attitude of rightously indignant innocence. Even when admitting to the full range of their abusive behaviors, they may avoid responsibility by minimizing the seriousness of the consequences to their daughters and families, or they may acknowledge the consequences but attribute them to the intercention of outsiders.

Indicators that a Child/Adolescent
May Have Experienced Sexual Abuse

The following list summarizes the behaviors we have discussed in this chapter as associated with family sexual abuse of children:

1. Depression
2. Withdrawal—e.g., child with few friends
3. Isolation from peers
4. Drug/alcohol abuse
5. Chronic runaway
6. Increase in physical complaints—e.g., headaches, miscellaneous illnesses

7. Attention-getting behavior—inappropriate acting out
8. Suicide attempts
9. Physical abuse—self-inflicted or inflicted by parents
10. Poor self-image—reflected in choice of clothing, overall appearance, cleanliness
11. Truancy—i.e., skipping school/classes
12. Drop in academic performance
13. Limited participation in organized social activities
14. Overly seductive behavior—Lolita Syndrome
15. Bi-sexual/homosexual experimentation
16. Repeated rape victim
17. Prostitution
18. Promiscuous sexual behavior
19. Heavy household responsibilities—e.g., regular responsibility for laundry, meal preparation
20. Overly restricted social activities

Behavioral Signs Among Young Children

1. Excessive masturbation
2. Encorpresis (fecal soiling)
3. Severe nightmares
4. Regression in developmental milestones
5. Explicit knowledge of sexual acts
6. Clinging/whining to a particular parent (non-abusive parent)
7. Open sexual behavior after age 5–7

Long-Term Psychological Effects on the Victim

Earlier we discussed personality characteristics by which incest victims could be identified. These characteristics are the psychological consequences of incest. The effects in adolescence include depression, acting out—including promiscuity—and confusion about sex. Lasting effects of incest are apparent in the longitudinal studies. Vestergaard (1960) contacted 16 incestuous daughters ten years after the termination of incest and concluded that the incestuous relations had been almost invariably damaging and sometimes resulted in pathological acting out.

Virginia Jacobson (1978), a clinical social worker, has commented on her observations on the long-term effects of incest. She states that the sexual experience with the father has profound negative effects on the development of a woman's identity and the results of the incest can include difficulty experiencing a nonsexual relationship with a man, continuing guilt and shame, and great anger.

When women are deprived of the experience of a non-sexual relationship with a man, they tend to see themselves as sex objects. They learn to use sex manipulatively and to trade it for extra favors. Their relationships with other women are affected as they perceive all women as sex objects of limited worth, whom they hold in contempt. They adopt a cynical, defensive, ambivalent stance vis-a-vis men. The limited scope of their experiences with men reinforces generalizations such as "all men are animals."

As a result of encountering society's shock and disapproval, the incest victim feels shame. The shame compounds the guilt she feels about taking her father from her mother and for receiving special favors and sometimes good erotic feelings from her father. Shame is particularly hard to treat as it involves a basic feeling of badness and hopelessness.

Women who have been sexually abused experience great anger. They feel that their dependency and powerlessness in relationship to their fathers have been exploited and used. They also experience enormous anger toward their mothers for not protecting them.

Women who were sexually abused as children and experienced no intervention exhibit a wide range of problematic behaviors in adulthood. Possible outcomes of incest include promiscuity, prostitution, complete aversion to sex, lesbianism (of a type seen as reactive to early sexual trauma), marital dysfunction, drug dependency, depression and suicide, and classic hysteria.

It has been found that a high percentage of women with sexual problems have a background of being sexually abused as children. Dr. James (1979) reports that sexual abuse especially incest, is a significant factor in the background of many young women who become prostitutes. Based on her research data, she estimates that the percent is between 17 and 22 percent. In reporting of the Chicago Vice Commission, 51 of 103 promiscuous women examined reported having had their first sexual experiences with their own fathers. In another study of 160 women who fell under the category of an individual "who cannot accept her own sexuality regardless of how she practices sex," it was found that 90 percent had been raped during childhood (Baisden, 1979).

Odyssey Institute surveyed 118 female drug abusers in New York and found that 44 percent of the women experienced incest as children (*Ms. Magazine,* 1977). At the Minnesota Correctional Institution for Women in Shakopee, Minnesota, it was found that 50 percent of the participants in an institution drug abuse program were incest or rape victims. (Shumate, 1978).

Even with intervention, the effects of early sexual trauma can remain. While at certain periods the former victim may function well and feel intact, at times of life or developmental crises the effect of incest can return with terrifying impact. The onset of adolescence, the decision to marry, the death of either parent, the onset of parenthood, and the developmental crises of the victim's children can all be periods of stress which reopen old wounds. Realistic intervention strategies include the recognition of the recurring nature of traumatic effects and the preparation of the victim to seek help for these as needed.

Chapter 18

Interviewing the Child
Sex Crime Victim

Although one researcher has estimated that more than one million American children are sexually assaulted each year, very few of these cases are brought to the attention of the police. The primary reason that child sexual abuse is a vastly under-reported crime is that frequently the victim and the offender are related. Family members may not report such sex crimes because of personal shame, misguided loyalty, fear of public exposure and embarrassment, or outright complicity. The child may not relate the abuse to anyone because she is naively obedient, fears retaliation, does not want to hurt the family, or is unaware that an offense has been committed.

Because of these factors, a great majority of incidents involving family members do not surface rapidly, if at all. Often, such cases of abuse represent long periods of chronic adult-child sexual activity, in which the child maintains genuine affection for the offender although she may have negative feelings about the sex acts. Some children may be active participants in sexual relations because of their need and desire for adult or parental affection and attention.

Child assaults committed by strangers are much more likely to be reported to the police. But even here, underreporting is prevalent because children often have difficulty in understanding and relating unusual experiences. Since the assault complaint is typically registered by the parents, they must first understand and believe the child's account.

The one background factor that seems common in cases of child sexual abuse is that the victims often come from a disorganized family. A recent study concluded that the great majority of sexual offenses occurred as a result of parental negligence. Three conditions of negligence were found to be typically involved: The daughter was in danger, the parent refused to listen to the child's story that she had been attacked or was in danger, or the parent was aware of the attack but took no positive action because a family member was the offender.

The study also showed that 33 percent of the child victims were from one-parent homes, and another 14 percent were from families where the parents were not legally married. Many of the children studied were victimized by members of their own family. For example, the report indicated that the girls between the ages of 6 and 15 were one and a half times more likely to be assaulted by a household member or blood relative than by a stranger.

Underreporting is not the only obstacle that the police face in dealing with child sex victims. Even when such assaults are reported, there frequently is a substantial time lag between the occurrence of the incident and the notification of the police. Many times the parent does not learn about the attack immediately because the child "forgets" to mention it. The victim may not think to mention the incident until something triggers her memory of it. For example, while being bathed, a young girl may remember the assault and tell her mother that someone had kissed or touched her. Police officers need to realize that a late report is often caused by the child's limitations in remembering and communicating experience. On the other hand, the longer the time period between the attack and the official reporting of it, the more difficult it is to investigate the case, and acquire evidence.

After the attack has been reported, police involvement in the case usually begins with the interview of the child. Interviewing a child is different from interviewing an adult, where both the officer and the victim are at last assured of "speaking the same language." The officer has to use special skills in conducting a successful interview of a child sex victim. He needs to have an insight into how children perceive and relate events, and he must have some understanding of the psychological reactions of the child and the parents to the incident.

Psychological Reactions

In cases of child sexual abuse, the police officer must consider carefully the emotional condition of the victim and her parents. An understanding of the various psychological reactions of the parents and child helps the officer to avoid causing unnecessary anguish and creates an atmosphere of trust and support, in which the investigative process, especially the initial interview, can proceed smoothly.

Parents

Child molestation is an offense where the emotions of the parents or guardians may be more complex and explosive than the psychological reactions of the victim. Because the child's emotional condition and attitude toward the police will likely reflect her parents' state, it is often necessary for the officer to consider the parents' reaction, if they are not involved in the offense, before concentrating on the victim.

Although parental reactions vary, there are typical emotional conditions for which the police officer can be prepared. Perhaps most common is the grief reaction, a combination of fear, anger, and sorrow. Here, the police officer should allow the parents to express or "ventilate" their feelings. After they have relieved some of their emotional tension, the officer should try to further calm the parents, assuring them that the child is safe and everything during the investigation will be carried out in her best interest.

Parents of child sex victims frequently experience feelings of extreme guilt. They blame themselves for "allowing" the assault to occur. Such expressions of guilt generally start with the word if—"if only I had moved to another neighborhood" or "if only I hadn't gone to the store." Where appropriate, the police officer should assure them that they have been responsible parents and that the only guilty party is the offender.

Sometimes the parents' guilt will be directed toward the child in the form of verbal abuse. The parents will blame the child for her misfortune. When this occurs, the police officer should separate the child from the parents and explain to them that their behavior will adversely affect the child's present condition and future recovery. Explanations such as these should be delivered tactfully, for the success of the interview and the well-being of the victim depend greatly on the rapport established between the police and the parents.

If one parent is the offender and the other parent's guilt is justified—for example, when a mother has known for some time about relations between her husband and daughter—the officer should acknowledge the mother's feelings but not criticize her behavior. Antagonizing the mother will only make interviewing the child a more difficult task.

Child

Many factors influence the emotional reactions that child sex victims have, and they must be taken into account, especially when trying to speculate about the long-range impact of the incident on the child's emotional health. The immediate goal of the police officer, however, is to calm and protect the victim from further emotional damage while carrying out the investigative interview.

The child may exhibit fear, embarrassment, guilt, or confusion. Emotional shock, manifested by crying, shaking, and restlessness, is a reaction that police officers frequently encounter. In such cases, the officer and the parents must comfort the child until her sense of well-being is restored.

Withdrawal is another common psychological reaction in these situations. The child may refuse to converse with the officer or to become involved in the interview in any other way. Embarrassment, a desire to forget the incident, or unfamiliarity with the interview surroundings and procedures may be at the root of this feeling. Patience and understanding on the part of the police officer will help the victim overcome these inhibiting fears.

When the offender is a family member or brutality is involved, the child may "repress" the incident and not be emotionally capable of discussing it. Repression is sometimes called "active forgetting" in that individuals will not allow themselves to remember unpleasant experiences. All that the police officer can do in this situation is to make the victim feel comfortable and secure and explain the importance of the interview in the hope that she will respond positively.

Particularly among older children, there may be guilt feelings associated with the assault. The child may feel that she somehow provoked the attack by her behavior. The guilt association may be quite childish; for example, the victim accepted candy or a ride from a stranger and then was "punished" for doing what her parents constantly warned her not to do. Or the victim's guilt may take a more adult form, such as wondering whether her own sexuality somehow enticed the offender. In any case, the police officer must make it completely clear that the child was not at fault and should not in any way hold herself responsible for what occurred.

Younger children may be genuinely confused about the attack. The victim may know that something unusual occurred but not that something "bad" or significant took place. Here, the police officer should try to get the facts of the case without alerting the child to the seriousness of the attack. So long as the child looks upon the incident as only an "unusual" event, her chances of a complete emotional recovery are very good.

Then concept of "protection through innocence" should be recognized by police officers. The premise of the concept is that the young child, because of her lack of awareness of the social taboos violated, will not suffer a long-lasting emotional disturbance from a sexual assault. Although all child sex victims probably experience some degree of short-term psychological stress, most will not suffer from long-range emotional problems unless they are adversely affected by the reactions of adults.

The Interview

The interview of any victim of a sex crime is demanding work. The interviewing officer must obtain information from a victim who typically finds it difficult and unpleasant to recount the personal aspects of the crime. If the police officer does not exercise tact and compassion, not only does the interview fail as an investigative process, but also the victim may unnecessarily suffer emotionally. Although interviewing an adult victim is difficult, the interview of a child is more so. Problems of communication and identification between an adult officer and a child victim must be overcome. The task becomes even more complicated when the offender is related to the victim. When the officer is confronted with both problems in interviewing a child victim of a sexual assault, the difficulty is compounded and special attention is required.

Timing

The interview should take place as soon as possible after the incident is reported. The longer the time interval between the assault and the interview, the less able the child is to recall the attack and relate the details. The welfare of the child cannot, however, be sacrificed for investigative expediency. Since extensive questioning by more than one officer can cause the victim emotional trauma, it should be avoided when possible. However, detailed questioning by the officer responsible for the initial interview is, however, necessary to establish whether a crime was committed and to obtain the identity or description of the suspect. The following procedures should, therefore, be applied during both the preliminary and in-depth follow-up interviews.

Setting

The in-depth interview of the victim should not take place until after the child has been medically examined and treated and other physical needs have been met. Personal needs often include washing and changing clothing.

The interview should take place in a comfortable setting where the child feels secure. The setting should provide privacy. Places that are not free from interruptions, distractions, and noise are inappropriate for effective interviewing. A preferred location is the child's home, so long as it is not the site of the attack. It is familiar to the child and will provide the needed privacy. If an office is used, the officer should ensure that it meets basic requirements of the interviewing setting, and he should permit the child to become familiar with it before starting the interview.

It is often desirable that a female police officer conduct the interview of a child sex victim. This will depend on the age, sex, and feelings of the victim. In many cases, though, a policewoman will not be available. At these times, the officer should consider using the presence of a female nurse or social worker to facilitate the interview process. Although the nurse or social worker will not participate in the actual interview, her mere presence may be comforting to the child.

Parents as Observers

When one of the victim's parents is the suspected offender, it is usually most productive to interview the child without either parent being present. In these cases the child probably will be hesitant to discuss the attack if family members participate in or observe the interview.

Where a parent is not the perpetrator, the police officer should explain to the child's parents the purpose and structure of the questioning before the interview begins. The officer's attitude must convey a sympathetic understanding of the parents' position, and their cooperation should be openly solicited. Experience has shown that a child's initial reaction to an interview is influenced greatly by the attitude of the parents. When the parents feel secure and display cooperativeness, the child will likely behave in the same way.

Whether the parents should be present during the interview depends entirely on the specific circumstances of the case. Some children will be frightened and uncommunicative if their parents are not present; others will be reluctant to discuss the matter in front of their family. Generally, if the child requests that her parents be present, her wish should be complied with. The parents can be seated behind the child so that they do not interfere with the questioning. When the child does not want her parents present, they may be seated outside the room where they can observe but not overhear the victim. An interview room equipped with a two-way mirror can fulfill this requirement. In all cases, the interviewing officer will have to judge what arrangement is best, keeping the welfare of the victim uppermost in his mind.

Rapport

One of the most important elements of the interview is the officer's ability to establish a rapport with the victim. An effective means of accomplishing this is for the officer to question the child about herself. Most children like to talk about themselves. Questions concerning the child's hobbies, school friends, and activities will show the child that the officer is interested in her as a person. In this way, an informal and friendly relationship between the two can be developed, and, in addition, the child will become accustomed to answering personal questions. Once rapport is established, the officer should be able to smoothly lead into discussion of the assault.

Obtaining the Statement

In all interviewing, child or adult, the police officer should let the victim describe the incident in her own words and should not ask detailed questions until the victim's statement is complete. The officer should listen attentively and encourage conversation with supporting gestures and comments. By nodding his head, the officer lets the child know that he is listening and understands what she is saying. Another way to encourage conversation is to repeat key words and the last word or statement that the child has made. Expressions such as "you feel that," "you are saying that," and "what you are trying to tell me" also help to draw out information.

The language the officer uses must suit the age and level of development of the child being interviewed. It is important that the officer stay on the child's level and phrase his questions in a language that the victim understands. Young children usually do not know the correct words for various parts of the body, especially sexual organs. When referring to some parts of the body, for example, children often use nicknames. The officer should ask the parents for the meanings of these nicknames and his report should reflect the terms used by the child and include the meaning attached to them by the victim. With older children, the officer's choice and manner of language will often be that of an adult. When talking to adults about sexual relationships, adolescents typically use formal language. Girls for instance, prefer formal language to child or street talk when discussing the topic of sex because it is less likely to embarrass them.

Because the purpose of the interview is to determine the facts of the crime, the police officer must question the victim about the details of the assault. Some details are not common knowledge among children, and they frequently cannot describe sexual activities in a vivid way. In addition, children sometimes find it difficult to distinguish between what actually happened and what they imagined to have occurred. This is especially true when the experience is a very emotional one. In overcoming these interview obstacles, the police officer relies on past experience, exercises patience, and seeks the advice of the victim's parents.

Victim Evaluation

During the interview, the police officer has to establish the potential of the child as a credible witness as well as determine the truthfulness of the child's statement. This evaluation is aimed at two characteristics of the victim; her ability to accurately relate the event and to distinguish between fantasy and truth.

The child's capacity to recall and relate information can be tested by asking her personal questions. Information should be solicited from her about family life, friends, school, and other interests. General questions about the community in which she lives, such as church and recreational activities, also help to determine her level of intellectual development. The child's replies to these questions not only help in evaluating the child's ability, but also the discussion serves as a means of fostering a rapport.

The victim's ability to tell time is often a crucial factor in establishing when the attack occurred. Questions about the hours and days of the week the child attends school will aid in this evaluation. There are other routine functions in the child's life which the officer can use to determine the time of the offense including television schedule, eating habits, and daylight and night time activities.

Whether the child can differentiate between the truth and a lie needs to be assessed by the interviewing officer. The officer should ask the victim if she knows the difference between the two and what happens when she tells a lie. The victim's answer may be expressed in child terms, but the important thing is her attitude. She should consider telling the truth as being positive and telling a lie as being negative. If there is a need, the police officer can verify the child's reputation for honesty by talking with the parents, teachers, friends and parents of friends.

Ending the Interview

The police officer should never end an interview abruptly. When he has obtained all of the facts about the incident, the officer should ask the child whether there is anything else she wishes to say. The child should be told that, if she remembers anything else about the assault, she should tell her parents. If the child is old enough to understand, the officer can explain the investigative steps to be followed.

The police officer should explain to the parents that the child may have to repeat her story to others, including the prosecutor, as well as testify in court. The parents should also be told that, if the case goes to trial, the police will help prepare the child for the courtroom hearing so that the experience will not be emotionally traumatic.

The parents should be cautioned against questioning the child about the incident. The less the child has to think about the assault, the faster her emotional recovery will probably take place. If the child wants to discuss the matter, however, the parents should be advised to talk about it frankly and without embarrassment.

Sometimes child sex victims and their families experience long-range emotional difficulties. Depending on the circumstances, the police officer may suggest that they seek the help of an appropriate social service agency, family physician, psychologist, or clergyman.

Preparing the Child for Court

When the investigation of a child sex offense ends successfully and a trial is scheduled, the police should begin to prepare the child for court. The officer should explain to the child courtroom procedures and the role of the judge, jury, prosecutor, and defense attorney. This explanation must be in such a manner that the child understands it. Where possible, the officer and the prosecutor should familiarize the child with the courtroom. She should be taken to the courtroom and allowed to sit in the judge's chair, at the attorney's table, and in the witness chair. The victim should also be familar with where she and her parents will be sitting. By acquainting the victim with the legal proceedings, the officer accomplishes two goals. He makes the child a better witness by reinforcing her self-confidence and makes the courtroom experience less mysterious and frightening.

Summary

For a variety of reasons, sexual crimes against children often go unreported. When a case of child molestation is brought to the attention of the police, the interviewing officer is responsible for obtaining the facts so that a proper investigation of the matter can be conducted. But interviewing a child sex victim is a very difficult and delicate assignment. The officer must consider the psychological condition of the victim and her family, gain the cooperation of the parents, and question the victim without causing her additional emotional problems. He must evaluate the victim in terms of her potential as a witness, and, if the case goes to court, the officer must prepare her for the trial.

Chapter 19

Child Prostitution: "Not for Sale"

When child abuse is discussed, it is addressed in terms of "non-accidental" injury or physical harm or beating, burning, etcetera. It may be discussed as "unfit homes," unfortunate circumstances," or "a sad state of affairs." It is unlikely in any case, that abuse would include the sexual motivations of adults as they relate to exploitation and commercialization, unless incest is discussed. Rarely do we talk about the prostituting child.

Physical and emotional harm which arises from the use of children in sexual acts which expose the child as a "sexual toy" inferring their involvement with adults can only speak to prostitution. Remember, a child who participates in pornography prostitutes himself or herself. It has become apparent in not only this country, but the majority of the world, that the use of children in this regard although denounced generally be society, is very simply, socially and economically rewarding to many. The use of children between two years of age and adulthood (commonly 18 years of age) is big business. It often involves persons of prominence, millions of dollars, and even parents of many youngsters.

Kiddie prostitution is defined as the use of, or participation by children—in sex acts for payment. Unlike the more common and traditional forms of child abuse, prostitution because of its "fee arrangement," engenders very often a willing participant. This in contrast, to the child-victim of beating, burning, or life in an unfit home.

Sometimes, say many persons of a more liberal consciousness, the children make a decision to participate freely. The contention that a two, three, four or even eight year old decides to participate freely, is rather doubtful.

The prostitution enterprise involving children is closely related to "Kiddie Porn," and both have a "second cousin" very often in incest.

It is "guesstimated" in a myriad of studies done in all areas of the United States, that the number of children involved in sexual exploitation exceeds one million. Recently, at the Sixth National Conference

133

of Juvenile and Family Court Judges, Mr. Steve F. Hutchinson, an authority on child prostitution stated that; "figures lead us to a conservative extrapilation of over a half million youngsters under the age of sixteen involved in "sex for sale."

All too often the abused, abandoned, and ambivalent child in today's society chooses prostitution as an alternative to what already seems an ugly reality. The wayward and the runaway can easily support themselves by "selling their bodies." As an estimate, a child in an area where this type of activity is desired would have no problem scoring from $100 to $200 per day, and even more if he has a manager, commonly called a "pimp."

The more rural the neighborhood or community the less the money from acts but the better the chances often times for recruitment, or the opportunity to work the commuter highways from one destination to another.

These children learn to "trick" for survival, having been duped into their position with promises of love, fun, reward, and even the opportunity of becoming a movie star or meeting celebrities that hold children of this sort in high regard for their individuality. Too often, the abuse of substances and many times suicide are the result of child prostitution. These children are considered nothing more than "fresh meat" by their human carnivores.

Prostituting children soon learn that although they are somewhat indispensable to the marketplace, they won't last forever. If they cannot impress their clients with alterations in fantasy, new positions for sexual gratification, or project that "sweetness" image, they are worth little. "Do you have a cherry for me?" is just one of the questions that children hear and must act to. Some youngsters may place plastic bags of blood in their vagina or anus to give the illusion of virginity or newness. Many of the "old ones" are used in rituals that are satanical or sadomasochistic in nature. At this juncture a child has virtually come to the end of the road.

Physical injury, mental and emotional impairments, and disease are the real rewards. The child's entire world is turned upside down. Ruined by middle class individuals rather than sex deviants. Middle-class people so often depicted as "dirty old men," "weirdos," and the like. Ruined by individuals who have forced children into acts of behavior known as adamism, exhibitionism, coprophalia, urolagnia, amphibulation, fellatio, cunninglus, annalingus, sodomy and triolism.

We would all do well to consider the "RIGHTS OF CHILDREN" and vehemently oppose their sexual exploitation. Children have no predisposition to be subjected to sexual exploitation, and more particularly child prostitution, but where money is the issue many children need a social reinforcement to resist being victimized.

Chapter 20

The Community Response: A Model

ON DEVELOPING A COMMUNITY DEMONSTRATION PROJECT SUGGESTIONS AND RECOMMENDATIONS

I. Demonstration Project Approach

Demonstrations seem safer to people than programs because (theoretically) "if you don't like the demonstrator you don't have to buy it." Of course, good salesmen present a product in ways to enhance desirability and hopefully to insure acceptance. Demonstration programs are a useful way to introduce news ideas or test new ways of doing things.

II. Leadership

Core leadership persons should be involved from the beginning in developing a project. It is essential that they understand the basic concepts and are better able to operationalize them as the project is developed. It is important to involve both citizens and professionals in the core leadership for innovation and change. These persons must, in combination, possess social change knowledge and skills, community knowledge, and have influence with other professionals and citizens.

III. Problem Definition

Who defines problems and how resources are assessed largely determines the goals of the project, and the strategies or methods. Choose social change rather than behavior change oriented persons.

IV. Resources

The intent was to develop a model which could be duplicated using resources currently existing in most rural areas. Therefore, we suggest that communities not use their time and resources seeking outside grants or funding.

Resources are what you need; not more money. Money can get resources for you but it could be better not to have much money. Grants and special funding can be a handicap because people and agencies end to see money and say, "Let them do the work—they got the money." This can be instant death or self-help and community development programs which are successful to the extent that many people work together without envy or competition for the control of resources or jobs.

Community self-help projects should use available technical assistance (from Universities and specialist professionals) with care. Community professionals and citizens must be the leaders, not the consultants. Select consultants who respect rural people and are willing to learn as well as be teachers, for rural programs need to be developed on the actual realities of rural life as well as on social science concepts.

We suggest that you consider trying the barter system as a way of bringing together the necessary resources for a child abuse and neglect program. It could work like this:

First Step—Bring together key persons to identify problems and plan program. Get concensus that program goals and strategies—go slowly enough to be sure there is sufficient common purpose and agreement.

Second Step—Determining what resources are needed. There will include such things as:

1. Personal—Project Staff
   a) project coordinator—full or part-time
   b) self-help organizers—full or part-time
   c) clerical help

Project Teams and Committees
   a) Citizens Committee for Children's Rights (see page 00 for recommendations) (This will largely be volunteer)
   b) Child Abuse and Neglect Study Team—(Professionals might be loaned personnel for a determined amount of time.)
   c) Inter-agency Council or Committee on Child Abuse and Neglect (Barter process could provide some competition between agencies for selection of competent and qualified representatives)

138

2. Other Expenses

Paper and materials, perhaps telephone and office space, etc. can be gathered by asking contributions of materials or monies or even having a bake sale.

The use of the barter system to obtain services involves the collection of resources from agencies, institutions, individuals, civic groups. One agency might loan a staff person full or part-time (be careful to write clear job descriptions and qualifications, for the fate of the programs can depend on the quality of staff.) It is difficult, if not impossible, to overcome the handicap of incompetent staff. Maybe there will be a skilled retired professional who will accept a staff position. Make certain that it is clear they joined up for the duration, that they are unpaid professionals not unpaid volunteers, and that they are "employed" to provide staff services.

Chapter 21

Building a Community Response to Child Abuse and Maltreatment

by Douglas J. Besharov, J.D., LI.M.

Child abuse is a hurt to all communities. Children from all racial, religious, social and economic groups are its victims. Abuse and maltreatment are symptoms of a society in trouble—a society in which the individual is dehumanized and the family is disintegrating.

New stories daily remind us of the horrors of child abuse and maltreatment. Nationwide, public agencies receive over 300,000 reports of suspected child abuse or maltreatment every year, and each year 2,000 children die in circumstances in which abuse or maltreatment is suspected. But no one knows for sure how many more children suffer harsh and terrible childhoods without their plight being detected and reported to the authorities.

Everyone pays the price of a young child's suffering. From the most practical as well as the most humanitarian points of view, it is less expensive and more humane to protect and nurture these children within the rehabilitated family environment than it is to endure the social costs of their continued abuse and maltreatment.

Unless we take compassionate yet firm steps to improve their plight, we consign these children to a life of continuing deprivation and peril. And we consign our communities to a future of aggression, drug abuse and violence.

Abused children often grow up to be socially destructive—to vent on others, particularly their children, the violence and aggression their parents visited upon them. As New York City Family Court Judge Nanette Dembitz rightly said: "The root of crime in the streets is neglect of children."

As a society, we have provided a combination of laws and procedures through which professionals and private citizens who come in

Douglas J. Besharov, J.D., LI.M., is director, National Center on Child Abuse and Neglect, Children's Bureau, OCD. His article is based on a speech delivered at the Louisville Child Abuse Coloquium in May 1975. It was prepared with the assistance of Nancy Fisher and Jose Alfaro.

contact with endangered children can, and in some situations must, take protective action. Laws have established reporting procedures, authorized the taking of children into protective custody and assigned child protective responsibilities to social agencies and the police. Laws have also created juvenile and criminal court jurisdictions and fostered treatment programs—all to protect vulnerable children and families.

But in almost every community in the nation, there are inadequacies, breakdowns and gaps in the child protective process. Detection and reporting are haphazard and incomplete; protective investigations are often poorly performed; and suitable treatment programs exist more in grant applications than in practice.

For far too many endangered children, the existing child protection system is inadequate to the life-saving tasks assigned it. Too many children and families are processed through the system with a paper promise of help. For example, as many as three-quarters of those children who die in circumstances in which abuse or maltreatment is suspected were known to the authorities before their deaths.

More fundamentally, prevention is an easily touted though little understood and unevenly pursued goal. Existing child protective procedures treat child abuse and maltreatment only after the fact, not on a primary preventive level. As we pointed out ten years ago, "preventing neglect and battering depends in the long run on preventing transmission of the kind of social deprivation which takes children's lives, damages their physical health, and retards their minds, and which contributes through those who survive to a rising population of next generation parents who will not be able to nurture children."

The challenge we face is not so much to discover what works; to a great extent we know what works. We must now discover how to develop the cooperative community structures necessary to provide needed services efficiently, effectively and compassionately.

According to conventional wisdom, the failure of our child protective institutions is caused by a dreadful lack of facilities, protective workers, social workers, judges, shelters and probation workers, and of all sorts of rehabilitative, social and psychiatric services. Undoubtedly, if we poured more millions of dollars into existing programs, the picture would be less bleak. But existing facilities and services, if properly utilized, could go a long way toward fulfilling the need to protect children.

Rehabilitative services are delivered by a social service system that is fragmented, overlapping and uncoordinated. If such diversity and competition created better services for children and their families, the lack of focus and unity in the system would not be of great concern.

But the result of such fragmentation has been blurred responsibility, diluted resources and uncoordinated planning, all of which severely limit the effectiveness of the overall approach. Local child protective agencies, police, juvenile courts, hospitals and a variety of other public and private agencies share, divide and duplicate scarce resources. The waste in manpower, expertise, record keeping, administration and policy planning cause by the existing fragmentation of services was never justified. It cannot now be tolerated in this period of severe budgetary constraint.

The patchwork complex of agencies and laws with divergent philosophies and procedures that makes up the average community's child protection system has been widely criticized. Responsibility is frequently passed from one agency or individual to another. Anywhere from three to eight agencies can be involved in a particular case. This means that three to eight separate individuals must become acquainted with the case, three to eight separate sets of forms must be filled out, three to eight referrals are made—all offering the possibility of administrative or bureaucratic fumbling.

The result is a system that limits the involvement of individuals and makes them powerless. As Dr. Ray Helfer has complained, often no one person is responsible and no one person is accountable. Additional consequences of fragmentation are frequent losses of information—situations in which one agency has critical information concerning a child's care or condition which is not communicated to the "appropriate" agency. Compounding this fragmentation and lack of involvement is a general absence of follow-up of referrals among agencies. One can well appreciate the frightful reality of endangered children "falling between the cracks."

While present efforts to prevent and treat child abuse and maltreatment are of limited effectiveness, the potential for helping families meet their child care responsibilities is great.

Children can be protected and their well-being fostered by helping parents to "parent." There are programs in all parts of the nation helping parents cope with the stresses of family life in our modern society. Social casework, psychological and psychiatric services, child abuse teams, lay therapists, parent surrogates, day care, Parents Anonymous groups, homemaker services, education for parenthood, and a whole range of other services and programs can and do make a difference in the level of family functioning. Unfortunately, these successful programs often are not seen as part of the child protection process in most communities. Either they are not available to protective services or they are not used. To fail to involve these family building programs in the protective process is to ignore an approach that can and does make an improvement in the level of family functioning.

Treatment is a community process. Without the use or, when necessary, the development of diverse, indigenous and, therefore, responsive programs, we consign the child protective process to the abusive removal of children from their homes, the overuse of foster care and the futility of treatment during brief bimonthly home visits.

Prevention, too, is a community process. It is necessary to incorporate into our individual, family and community life a greater understanding of family hygiene. A renewed sense of respect or the human growth of all individuals within the context of the family would do more to lower violence and aggression against the young than any number of social agencies which can become involved only after the process of family breakdown has progressed almost past the point of irremediable damage.

Public Support

Though the efforts of concerned professionals are indispensable to the coordination and improvement of services, the key to real progress is an informed and aware citizenry. Child abuse and maltreatment are not few problems but, traditionally, the moving force for the development of treatment and preventive programs has existed largely in the professional community. Broad based public support—crucial for the funding of programs and the breaking of bureaucratic logjams—has been missing. Although sympathetic citizens have been enraged and shocked by the inherent sensationalism of individual child abuse and maltreatment cases, until very recently overall public awareness, understanding and support have been sporadic and unfocused.

When exposed to an abused child, the first reactions of most people are utter disbelief, denial and avoidance. Finding the cruel and tragic condition of the child beyond their capacity to understand, they deny that the injury was deliberately inflicted or that a parent could be responsible. They deny the horror of a child's home environment and the probability that the child and his siblings had been battered previously. Even more painful, people meeting with such children evade their own responsibility, explaining "I don't want to get involved"; "It's not my job"; "I don't want to come between the child and his parents"; or "Don't ask me to report a parent to the authorities—that would be interfering with the privacy and rights of the family."

Because of the tremendous publicity generated by numerous sensational cases in communities across the nation, we are reaching a time when the public can no longer refuse to see the evidence for what it is—that children do suffer almost unbelievable harm at the hands of their parents.

Now, there is a danger that denial will turn to outrage and overreaction. Upon confronting child abuse, citizens as well as some professionals sometimes act as if they have discovered absolute evil.

The reality of child abuse is so awful that a harsh, condemnatory response is understandable. But such reactions must be tempered if any progress is to be made. If we permit feelings of rage towards the abusers of children to blind us to the needs of the parents as well as of the children, these suffering and unfortunate families will be repelled and not helped. Only with the application of objective and enlightened policies can treatment, research, prevention and education be successfully performed.

Hitherto, the publicity attached to spectacular cases has served to educate the public and professions to the existence and nature of the problem. Henceforth, the burden will be on concerned members of society to devise procedures for the protection of these unfortunate youngsters through the rehabilitation and strengthening of their families. There must now be a reversal in the attitude of the public toward parents who have been seen as cruel perpetrators. In the words of Dr. Vincent J. Fontana, "We must come to realize that there are two victims of child abuse—the child and the parent."

Mounting public awareness now needs to be sharpened and developed into a constructive, effective force for far-reaching reform. An intensive national public service campaign on child abuse and maltreatment can meet prejudices, emotionalism and misunderstanding head on. Sympathy for abused and maltreated children must be channeled into constructive help in their behalf.

All citizens must recognize the critical need to strengthen the family so that it can better cope with periods of stress. The public must come to understand that in certain circumstances almost any family can have difficulty coping and that, at such times, the family members must be able to seek and find help. Only if this level of understanding is reached can public concern be channeled into true community action.

Child abuse laws provide only the legal and institutional framework for action. A law lives in the way it is used. Child abuse and child maltreatment are family and community problems. If we are to prevent and treat them, we must have a community commitment to fostering the emotional and behavioral hygiene of the individual, the family and the community.

Child abuse must be understood as a function of uncontrolled or uncontrollable personal, familiar and social stress. Despite popular misconceptions, most abusing parents are not sadists, criminals or mentally retarded persons. Abusing parents are capable of loving the children they harm and they often experience great guilt and remorse about their abusive behavior. In many ways, they are like all parents. But when they experience moments of anger and frustration, they are likely to take it out on their children. Sometimes they confuse discipline with the expression of their own inner fury.

All parents and parents-to-be can benefit from family-life education and a knowledge of child development. Parenting is not instinctive, and experts have learned a great deal about child rearing that needs to be communicated to parents. As a first step, parents must be taught that when they are under stress their children can be in danger.

The abusing or imminently abusing parent must be reached. Parents who have problems in rearing their children are acutely sensitive to being labeled sick, sadistic or degenerate. They also fear punishment and jail. If these parents sense this attitude in treatment programs, they will pull away, further endangering their children, or forcing a protective agency to remove a child from his home. A truly rehabilitatively oriented social system must create an understanding atmosphere, even though further abuse or maltreatment cannot be condoned.

Often these parents are the most difficult to reach, for they are usually isolated people, fearful of the possible community response to their behavior. But they must be reached and told that help is available—help that can enable them to better meet their parenting responsibilities, keep the family together and protect the child within the family home. Parents need to be told where they can seek help, including help from family service agencies, child protective agencies, self-help groups, doctors, visiting nurses, day care programs, clergy, neighbors, friends and family. They need to be assured that someone cares, that someone is willing to help them when they need help. But if we expect troubled families to come forth, the help offered them must be real.

Prevention and treatment are a community responsibility. We know that there are many current programs which have demonstrated that they can successfully help parents care for their children and maintain family life. Every community must take inventory to see whether it has the basic ingredients for a comprehensive, indigenous and responsive program to meet local needs for the prevention and treatment of child abuse and maltreatment and to aid parents in stress.

Over 100 years ago, Emerson wrote: "If a man can write a book, preach a better sermon, make a better mousetrap . . . the world will make a beaten path to his door." So too, if we build community resources that better help families function, families in need will beat a path to their doors.

Appendix

Bibliography of Audio-Visual Aids

Child Abuse and Neglect Resource Center
Department of Special Education
California State University, Los Angeles
5151 State University Drive
Los Angeles, CA 90032
(213)224-3283

COMPILED BY: REGION IX CHILD ABUSE
NEGLECT RESOURCE CENTER

1/79

Films

Don't Give Up on Me (28 min. 16 mm, color)
Produced for the Metropolitan Area Protective Services, and the Illinois Department of Children and Family Services for use in caseworker awareness training, the program uses real people in real situations to probe the reasons behind the child abuse pattern. Included are recreated scenes from a case history and scenes from actual counseling workshops. In addition to its primary audience, the program is designed for mental health agencies, social work oriented college curricula, health care centers, law enforcement agencies, libraries, civic groups, and the concerned public.

War of the Eggs (27 min.)
A young lawyer and his wife pace restlessly in a hospital waiting room as their two year old son, critically injured from a fall, undergoes emergency surgery. Both claim it was an accident. A hospital psychiatrist, seeking to determine the cause of the fall, is dubious. He says X-rays reveal the child has a chronic history of such injuries. Under his gentle probing, the truth emerges. At breakfast, they quarreled bitterly. As a result, the child started to cry. Enraged, she pushed him

149

down a flight of stairs. Admitting this, they expose their real problem; self-hatred. Slowly, painfully, they open up to each other, take responsibility for what they have done and face the fact that they need help. A sensitive exploration of the child battering syndrome.

Fragile: Handle with Care (narrated by Bill Cosby) (26 min.)

This film has been dedicated to children all over the world. It depicts the battering parent, the results of child abuse, and the help society can offer, by focusing in on three families. The situations you will see are all re-enactments of authentic case histories.

Cipher in the Snow (24 min.)

The true story of a little boy no one thought was important until his sudden death one snowy morning. A film to motivate concern for the needs of every child.

Cradle of Violence (20 min.)

This film is about the problem of child abuse, and solutions to the frustrations of parenthood that bring about violence against children. The film gets actual child abusers to explore their problems. The tone of the film is very positive and provides motivation to continue to help with the problems whether they are professional personnel or concerned citizens. It is a documentary film designed for school, library, church, and community group programs.

Children in Peril (narrated by Marlene Sanders) (22 min.)

This film takes the viewer on a provocative tour of several agencies and hospitals throughout the United States where child abuse cases are treated. At Denver General Hospital, Dr. C. Henry Kempe states that child abusers are not much different from ordinary parents or adults. What causes one to step across the line and become a child abuser? The camera scans "therapy groups" revealing the emotions and thoughts of child abusers. Also discussed in this film are the legal implications of child abuse.

Mother-Infant Interaction (35 min.)

Series of taped delivery room interactions, depicting the very first encounter between mother and child. This will demonstrate one technique for the early indentification of not only normal behavior, but that which may indicate potential problems with mother-child interaction.

Incest: The Victim Nobody Believes

Vincent de Francis, the director of the Children's Division of the American Humane Association, says that the incidence of sexual abuse is "many times greater" than that of physical abuse. Yet in comparison with society's efforts for the battered child, the sexual abuse victim has been virtually ignored. Incest is a taboo; people do not talk about it. As the first film to openly discuss the issues of sexual abuse/misuse, this film breaks down this taboo to make the public aware of the extent of the problem and recognize the impact a childhood incestuous experience can have on a victim's entire life.

The Interview (35 min.)

This film presents an actual interview between a parent of a suspected abused child and a physician. The film demonstrates important interviewing principles for the medical interview, and outlines one approach to gathering important medical, social, and psychological information with which to conduct an assessment and treatment plan. In the discussion session after the film, the group is encouraged to review the film's content, trainee reactions to and feelings about the film, and the interview process demonstrated.

Abusive Parents (30 min.)

This film includes excerpts from a panel discussion by four women incarcerated at the California Institite for Women for crimes involving child abuse, followed by an interview with Else Ten Broeck, founder and former director of a therapeutic day care center for abused children and their families. The interview covers the social context of abuse, personal and family dynamics that may contribute to abuse, and a generic profile of abusers.

Investigating Reports of Child Abuse and Neglect (26 min.)

This film dramatizes investigations of 1) a reported incident of alleged physical abuse, and 2) a report of an unsupervised child. The film presents comments from practitioners who are responsible for investigation reports of child abuse and neglect.

Working Together *(30 min.)*

The film consists of interviews with members of multidisciplinary teams or councils in three different communities: San Diego, California (a small, coastal city); Montgomery County, Maryland (an affluent suburb of Washington, D.C.); and Salina, Kansas (the county seat of a rural midwestern county). These communities cover the range and sizes and types of communities that have developed and can develop effective multidisciplinary approaches.

Presenting the Case *(30 Min.)*

Trainees view a film that shows a social worker testifying in a juvenile court child abuse hearing. A narrator critiques the testimony, highlighting major points. Following the film trainees discuss examples of rules of evidence, rules of testimony, and cross-examination.

The Medical Witness *(35 min.)*

The film portrays a physician carrying out the various functions involved in testifying as an expert medical witness in a juvenile court child abuse case. The doctor is seen in a pre-trial interview with the county attorney assigned to present the case in court, and later as an expert witness at the adjudictory hearing. A narrator highlights the main points made by the film's dramatizations.

Sexual Abuse *(30 min.)*

This film provides an overview of intra-family sexual abuse of children: what it is, common myths, physical and behavioral indicators, family dynamics, how to conduct examinations and investigations with a minimum amount of psychological damage to the child, and different approaches to the problem among various professionals.

Initial Interview *(25 min.)*

Illustrates techniques useful in conducting a diagnostic which elicits necessary information and establishes a treatment relationship.

The Social Context of Child Abuse *(10 min.)*

Identifies and illustrates the social norms which promote and perpetuate the phenomena of child abuse and neglect.

Treatment Techniques (Part 1 and 2)

Simulated vignettes illustrates a series of specific treatment techniques by showing brief worker/client interactions. Techniques useful with low self-esteem, with denial, with limit setting and with therapy groups are presented.

Borderline Case Conference and Borderline Case Conference Follow-Up

Presents the core conference which includes parents and all involved professionals as a model for successful case coordination around decision-making, planning and follow-up.

Case Conference Including Parents (25 min.)

This film presents the conference of all involved professionals and abusive parents, as models for diagnosing and assessing cases of child abuse.

Physicians in Court (30 min.)

Illustrates what a physician may expect when testifying in Juvenile Court and presents the pre-hearing conference with the Court representative as crucial preparation for this.

This Child Rated X (45 min.) (Part 1 and 2)

This film examines the Juvenile Justice system in America. This Child Rated X looks into the correctional institution which houses juvenile offenders, and explores the feelings of both authorities and children in these institutions.

A Chain to Be Broken (45 min.)

Successful professionals give the viewer broad definitions and keen insight into both active and passive forms of abuse. The film highlights Parents Anonymous, a working solution for parents with abuse problems. A crisis house is presented to give insight to those who work with and for troubled families. A Trauma Council suggests alternatives for communities that suffer from fragmented delivery systems

Filmstrips

Medical Indicators of Abuse and Neglect (65 min.)

Five short filmstrips will be shown, each focusing on one of the following conditions: sexual abuse, neglect, and physical abuse as manifested by skin trauma, bone injuries, and internal injuries. Each filmstrip presents the medical indicators and special concerns to be aware of in diagnosing abuse and neglect.

Child Abuse and Neglect:
What the Educator Sees (15 min.)

Depicts physical and behavioral indicators of abuse and neglect which children are likely to display in a school setting. The filmstrip also discusses the unique vantage point that teachers and other educators have in identifying and responding to abused and neglected children.

Physical Indicators of Abuse,
Signs of Alert: Part A (13 min.)
Physical Abuse, What Behavior
Can Tell Us: Part B (14 min.)

An overview of physical and behavioral indicators of physical abuse. *Part A* looks at major external and internal physical manifestations of abuse. *Part B* looks at child behavior and interactions between children and parents which may indicate abuse.

Indicators of Neglect,
Before It's Too Late (12 min.)

Shows some typical forms of neglect and its behavioral and physical indicators. It raises the issue of child neglect as a serious problem, but one which is frequently difficult for professionals to identify—especially when it seems to involve differences among child-rearing practices in various cultural and socio-economic groups.

Issues in Reporting Child Abuse and Neglect (15 min.)

Dramatizes a variety of reasons child care professionals may be reluctant to report cases of suspected child abuse and neglect, followed by interviews with professionals in the child abuse field who suggest ways of information on the origin, purpose, and basic provisions of reporting laws.

Case Planning and Referral (15 min.)

Looks at case planning from both the family's and the professional's point of view. Using a case history, it examines the major problems encountered in each part of the process—assessment, treatment planning, and case monitoring—and presents some solutions to these problems that have improved the effectiveness of agency and individual efforts.

The Minority Child

These filmstrips are designed to provide clear sensitive insights into the needs of children from minority cultures.

This film series is divided into three parts, each part containing five sections.

1. **The Puerto Rican Child**
   a. The old home and the new
   b. Three generations
   c. Life with Puerto Rican parents
   d. The formative years
   e. Pride in belonging
2. **The Chicano Child**
   a. A chance for our children
   b. La Familia
   c. Responsibilities of parenthood
   d. Learning with the family
   e. From home to school
3. **The Black Child**
   a. The black child in America
   b. Racial awareness and problems
   c. The foundation of racial identity
   d. Black, proud, and able
   e. In behalf of our children

Slides

The Visual Diagnosis of Nonaccidental Trauma and Failure to Thrive (40 min.)

This slide presentation presents an overview of physical indicators of child abuse and/or neglect.

Medical Identification of Child Abuse and Neglect for Non-Physicans (30 min.)

(61 slides and audio-tape cassette) presents the various characteristic manifestations of abuse and neglect, briefly outlines necessary anatomy and delineates factors which determine index of suspicion.

Medical Identification of Child Abuse and Neglect for Physicians (30 min.)

(Fifty-nine slides and audio-tape cassette) presents the various characteristic manifestations of abuse and neglect, outlines determining index of suspicion, and details procedures and tests necessary to diagnosis.

Sometimes I Feel Like a Motherless Child: Joy Child (15 min.)

An example of a public information presentation that utilizes a visual approach to heighten awareness about the problem of child abuse and what can be done about it. The slides include settings that provoke abuse, examples of abused children, and normal family settings.

Diagnosis of Child Abuse and Neglect via Physical Findings (20 min.)

Narrative slide presentation dealing with various physical aspects of child abuse and neglect, including: bruises and welts, burns, central nervous system damage, bone injuries, and failure to thrive.

An Overview (8 min.)

Describes the development of public awareness of the problem of child abuse, the enactment of reporting laws by state legislatures during the 1960s and agencies which have been established to help the abused child and his parents.

Identification and Referral (25 min.)

Tells teacher, nurse, or counselor how to identify and refer an abused or neglected child according to the Texas Family Law Code.

Legal Aspects (10 min.)

An interview with Judge W. H. Miller of the Harris County Juvenile Court System in which the Judge answers questions administrators and teachers have about reporting laws and about permitting Child Welfare workers to interview and photograph abused children at school.

The Administrator's Role in Combating Child Abuse and Neglect
(10 min.)

Used by administrators to develop both board and administrative policies to initiate a program against child abuse and neglect. Information concerning reporting laws, immunity laws and the misdemeanor penalty for failure to report is presented, along with a suggested procedure for referring suspected cases of abuse or neglect.

Behavior of Parents and Children (Behavioral Vignettes)

This is a series of six slides, each suggest a story line to the viewer by means of the behavior depicted in the slides. Viewers are asked to interpret the pictures by making up stories to accompany each set of slides. This exercise is designed to give trainees experience in recognizing behaviors and interactions that could be indicative of child abuse and neglect.

Videotapes

Legal Response to Child Abuse by Los Angeles County Council

The Treatment of Father-Daughter Incest: A Psycho-Social Approach

Henry Giarretto, director of the Child Sexual Abuse Treatment Program discusses the approach taken in treating the incestuous family.

Audio Cassette

Dr. Helfer, of the College of Human Medicine, Michigan State University, presents a series of self-instructional audio-visual units. Useful to any individuals involved with abuse and/or neglect. Six audio-visual instructional programs in covering one or more aspects of abuse or neglect. Loose leaf manual accompanies the audio-cassette.

Unit 1 The World of Abnormal Rearing
Unit 2 Making Diagnosis of Child Abuse and Neglect in Small Children
Unit 3 This Unit Covers the Diagnostic Process

Unit 4 This Unit Covers the Theoretical Basis for Treatment Programs and Ways to Determine if the Home is safe for a Given Child
Unit 5 Developing Community Programs
Unit 6 Review

Child Abuse: Who Suffers, Who Cares?

Twelve audio-cassettes. The broadcast quality tapes provide in-depth coverage of a broad range of child abuse and neglect. Tract is 24 minutes long and covers a specific area of concern, discussed by people knowledgeable in that area.

Sexual Abuse (Tape 1 and 2 by Roland Summit)

Child Abuse English-Radio Spots

La Familia Sana (The Healthy Family) in Spanish (Ten Programs: 5 min. each)

Child Abuse and Harmful Discipline
Constructive Child Discipline (1)
Constructive Child Discipline (2)
Constructive Child Discipline (3)
The Effects of Marital Problems
Preparation for Marriage
The Danger of Early Marriage
The Self Actualization of Women (1)
The Self Actualization of Women (2)
The Self Actualization of Women (3)

These problems are especially suitable as starters for discussion groups and pastoral counseling sessions, and for use in high school classes on Marriage and Family Relations. The programs have already been enthusiastically received and used by Hispano professionals in the field of psychology, marriage counseling, child development, child abuse, youth work, drug abuse programs, neighborhood centers, and basic education for low-income mothers.

Consultants and Resources

Consultants/Lectures

James R. Davis, Criminologist, may be contacted by writing to 2387 Rippey Ct., El Cajon, CA 92020. He can be contacted by phone at 714-462-7354 or 805-544-7101 regarding his travel schedule and lecture series. Mr. Davis has a travel team available for seminars through the U.S.

Specialized Management Services Company, San Luis Obispo, CA. May be contacted for information on their twenty hour *"Child As Victim"* seminar. Approximate costs can be quoted by calling 805-541-1066.

Systems & Operational Services, (SOS), 339 El Portal, Pismo Beach, CA 93449, may be contacted regarding lecturers both in and out of California, slide-presentations, and film-production of training material. This firm has a five person travel team available for travel nationally, including a forensic odontologist.

Robert L. Tafoya, Consultant, *"Domestic Violence"* areas, 11351 Homeway Drive, Garden Grove, CA 92641. 714-539-1486.

Delinquency Control Institute of the University of Southern California, 3601 S. Flower St., Los Angeles, CA 90007. Specialized school offered called the *"Child Abuse Update."*

California Specialized Training Institute (C.S.T.I.) Bldg. 904, Camp San Luis Obispo, CA 93406. Juvenile Investigation Patrol Officers Seminars. Includes responses to abuse, neglect, incest, and sexual assult. Telephone 805-544-7101.

Books

Beyond the Best Interests of the Child, by *A. Freud; J. Goldstein; and A. Polnit. The Free Press,* 1973.

This book addresses the issues involved in removing the children from natural, foster, and common law, families. It states that the interviewer should identify 1) if the child is unwanted; 2) if the home is the least detrimental placement. All decisions should be made based on "the least detrimental effects" on the child, should be "continuous and unconditional," and should be based on the child's "time reference."

Child Abuse Interventions and Treatment. *Editors: Nancy B. Ebeling, MSSA; ACSW; Deborah A. Hill, MSW. Sponsored by: Children's Advocator, Inc. Publishing Sciences Groups, Inc. Action, Massachusetts, 1975.*

"This important work presents current views on social-medical problem that can be found in every stratum of our society . . . social workers, doctors, psychiatrists, nurses, probation officers, project directors, and attorneys discuss the multiplicity of child abuse problems. . . ." (from the book jacket).

Planning and Organizing for Social Change—Action Principles from Social Science Research, *by Jack Rothman. Columbia University Press, New York, 1974.*

In this book Rothman did a systematic review of the social sciences literature to provide social welfare planners and social workers social change concepts, strategies and actions.

Rights of Children, *by the Harvard Educational Review. Reprint Series No. 9, 1974, Massachusetts.*

"Selected articles demonstrating from the standpoint of the child, the institutions, policies, and professionals a child encounters. Presents the need to establish clearly the rights of the children." (Excerpt Preface)

Somewhere a Child Is Crying—Maltreatment-Causes & Prevention, *by Vincent J. Fontana, M.D. MacMillan, N.Y. 1973.*

An in-depth study of a national problem (child abuse) which outlines a concrete program for eliminating its causes. Diagnostic guidelines for teachers and neighbors who suspect child abuse and neglect. Suggested programs for schools, colleges, and social agencies.

The Children's Cause, *by Gilbert Y. Steiner. The Brookings Institution, Washington, D. C., 1976.*

" . . . this book examines the apparatus for making Children's policy and evaluates substantive policy proposals against the background of tension between proponents of public rather than private responsibility and between advocates of federal rather than state responsibility." (from the foreward).

Violence Against Children: Physical Child Abuse in the United States, *by David G. Gil. Harvard University Press, Cambridge, Massachusetts, 1970.*

"Violence Against Children . . . offers an opportunity to note briefly several developments reflecting a growing awareness of the rights of children." (From the preface.)

Incest: Confronting the Silent Crime, *430 Metro Square Bldg., St. Paul, Minnesota 55101.*

Child Abuse & Neglect Prevention and Treatment in Rural Communities, *DHEW Publication No. (OHDS) 78–30154—also may be obtained by writing: Family Service Assn., 364 High St., Morgantown, West Virginia 26505*

Manuals, Reports, Proceedings

The Legal Aspects of Child Abuse and Neglect, *by Barbara A. Caufield. Direct your request for this manual to: Mildred Arnold, Public Service Administration, Office of Human Development, Dept. of Health, Education & Welfare, Room 2014, South Buildings, Washington, D.C.*

"The focus of this manual was directed by the professionals who work daily with families." It outlines steps protective service workers must take for investigation, evaluation for court, trial, and disposition.

Child Maltreatment in the United States: A Cry for Help and Organizational Response, *by Saad A. Nagi. The Ohio State University, 1976. For a copy of this material write to: The Children's Bureau, Office of Child Development, Dept. of Health, Education and Welfare.*

"The purposes of the book were: 1) to gain an analytical, nationally representative picture of the organization of services with child abuse and neglect; 2) to indentify limitations and strengths in the structure and performance of these programs; and 3) to prepare recommendations for improving and controlling the problem" (p. 4).

Comprehensive Emergency Services: Community Guide, *by National Center for Comprehensive Emergency Service to Children. Copies may be obtained by writing: Patricia W. Lockett, Director, 320 Metro Howard Office Bldg., Nashville, Tennessee 37210.*

"This material was prepared . . . as a part of the National Center for Comprehensive E.S.C. Center's mission to prepare and disseminate mixed-media materials to communities interested in organizing and operating a coordinated system of 24-hour emergency services to children and their families." (from the Title Page).

Getting Human Services to People in Rural Areas, *by the Office of Rural Development, Office of Human Development HEW, Washington, D.C. 20501. (Copies may be obtained by writing the above address)*

"A study focused on field evaluations of ten rural projects supported by DHEW funds."

Towards A National Policy for Children & Families, *by Advisory Committee on Child Development, Assembly of Behavioral and Social Sciences. Copies may be obtained by writing National Research Council, 2101 Constitution Avenue, Washington, D.C., 20418.*

This report focuses attention on the need to develop a national policy for children and families to the problems they face on a daily basis.

Child Abuse and Neglect Programs, *by U.S. Dept. of HEW, Office of Human Development, Office of Child Development, Children's Bureau, National Center on Child Abuse and Neglect, Washington, D.C. (Copies may be obtained by writing the above).*

A listing of all child abuse and neglect programs in the Department of Health, Education, and Welfare Regions.

Child Abuse and Neglect, *by Maure Hurt, Jr. Social Research Group, The George Washington University, Washington, D.C. Copies may be obtained by writing U.S. Dept. of HEW, Office of Human Development, Office of Child Development, Washington, D.C. (Publications No. [OHD] 74–20.)*

"A report of the status of the research on child abuse and neglect:

National Institute for Advanced Studies: Draft Federal Standards on Prevention and Treatment of Child Abuse and Neglect. *600 E. St., N.W. Suite 100, Washington, D.C. 20004.*

Profile of Neglect, *by Norman A. Polansky, Carolyn Hally, and Nancy F. Polansky. Copies may be obtained by writing U.S. Dept. of HEW, Social Rehabilitation Service, Community Services Administration, Washington, D.C. (1975).*

A survey of the state of knowledge of child abuse and neglect.

Proceedings of the First National Conference on Child Abuse and Neglect, *by the Regional Institute of Social Welfare Research, Publication No. (OHD) 72–30094. Copies may be obtained by writing the Dept. of Health, Education and Welfare, Washington, D.C.*

"This volume is not intended to provide specific, in-depth information on the problem and its management. Rather its goal is to capture various conceptual threads that were cast at the conference." (from the Overview).

Child in Sport: Physical Activity, *National Conference Workshop. Editors, J. G. Albinson and G. M. Andrew, School of Psysical and Health Education, Queen's University, Kingston, Ontario, Canada. University Part Press, Baltimore, 1976.*

Organizations

The American Humane Association. *Children's Division, P.O. Box 1266, Denver, Colorado. Vicent DeFrancis, Director of Children's Division.*

"The Children's Division of the American Humane Association is the National Association of individuals and agencies working to prevent neglect, abuse and exploitation of children." (Newsletter and other publications.)

Child Welfare League of America, Inc. *67 Irving Place, New York, New York 10003.*

"The Child Welfare League of America is a federation of child welfare agencies. Its purpose is to protect and promote the welfare agencies and communities and provide essential social services for children and families. It sets standards, conducts research and publishes materials and promotes legislation to meet its purpose." (Newsletter and Publications)

Rural America, Inc. *Dupont Circle Building, 1346 Connecticut Avenue, NW, Washington, D.C.*

"A voice for small towns and rural people."—A Lobbying Group (Newsletter)

Regional Research Institute for Human Services. *Arthur G. Emlen, Director, Permanent Planning Project, Regional Research Institute for Human Services, Portland State University, P.O. Box 751, Portland, Oregon 97207. (Newsletter)*

Parents Anonymous, Inc. *2810 Artesia Boulevard, Redondo Beach, CA 90278.*

Parents Without Partners. *7910 Woodmount Avenue, Washington, D.C. 20014.*

"Through programs of discussions, professional speakers, study groups, newsletters, and international publications, real help is provided the confused and isolated to find himself and to reshape his own life to meet the unique and unpredictable conditions of single parenthood." (Newsletter)

The American Parents Committee, *Mrs. Helen K. Blank, Executive Director, 1346 Connecticut Avenue, NW, Washington, D.C. 20036, Telephone (202) 785-3169.*

"The APC invites the cooperation of many other national nonprofit organizations in striving for (a) better Federal Legislation for children and for (b) the more adequate funding of services for children and for (c) more effective administration of such services." (Newsletter)

Center for Comprehensive Emergency Services to Children in Crisis. *Patricia W. Lockett, Director, Room 320, 25 Middleton Street, Nashville, Tennessee 37210.*

(Newsletter: Cross Talk; Manual: Comprehensive Emergency Service)

Education Commission of the States: Child Abuse and Neglect Project. *300 Lincoln Tower, 1860 Lincoln Street, Denver, Colorado 80295, C.D. Jones, Director.*

(Report: Education for Parenthood)

Newsletters:

Concern—The National Victim/Witness Resource Center Newsletter. *P.O. Box 39045, Washington, D.C. 20016.*

Child Protection Report. *1301 20th St., NW, Washington, D.C. 20036.*

Criminal Justice Newsletter. *An N.C.C.D. Publication, 411 Hackensack Ave., Hackensack, New Jersey, 07601.*

Response: Violence and Sexual Abuse in the Family. *Center for Women, Policy Studies, 2000 P. St., NW, Washington, D.C. 20036.*

Order Form

Please send me copies of

	Quantity	Price
"Help Me, I'm Hurt: The Child Victim Handbook"	_____	_____
"Street Gangs: Youth, Biker, and Prison Groups"	_____	_____

☐ **Check enclosed** (Kendall/Hunt pays   ☐ **Bill me** (Plus shipping   ☐ **Charge my account:**
shipping and handling)   and handling)

Name _____

Affiliation _____

City _____ **State/ZIP** _____

Phone _____/_____

Charge my credit account: ☐ Visa ☐ Master card
Account No.   MC Bank #
☐☐☐☐☐☐☐☐☐☐☐☐☐☐☐☐☐ ☐☐☐☐
Exp. Date ____ Signature _____
(required for all charges)

Kendall/Hunt Publishing Company
2460 Kerper Boulevard • Dubuque, Iowa 52001